Wisdom

FOR PARENTS

A Daily Devotional from the Book of Proverbs

BY FRANK HAMRICK

PositiveAction
FOR CHRIST

Wisdom For Parents

Copyright © 2008 by Positive Action For Christ, Inc. P.O. Box 700, 502 W. Pippen Street, Whitakers, NC 27891-0700. All rights reserved. No part may be reproduced in any manner without permission in writing from the publisher.

Printed in the United States of America

ISBN: 978-1-59557-055-0

Edited by C.J. Harris

Layout and Design by Shannon Brown

Published by

Preface

Several years ago, I wrote a devotional entitled *Apples for Teachers* to encourage Christian educators to focus on reaching their students' hearts rather than merely teaching their heads. The book received such an enthusiastic response that I decided to produce an edition geared towards the home rather than the classroom. Changes have been made throughout, and several days have been entirely rewritten to include proverbs that focus specifically on family matters. It is with much excitement that I present Wisdom for Parents.

This book contains thoughts from the book of Proverbs that are an outgrowth of my personal devotional life and many years of experience as a parent and grandparent. Hopefully these thoughts will minister to your soul and be "an ornament of grace and chains about thy neck" (Prov. 1:9) to glorify God in your home. My prayer is that this book will be a daily reminder of what is truly important and will help focus your heart and your family's eyes upon our Lord.

Frank Hamrick
Rocky Mount, North Carolina

Day 1

PROVERBS 1:1
"The proverbs of Solomon, the Son of David, King of Israel."

Pithy Parents

Interestingly, the wisest human who ever lived spoke in proverbs. Solomon understood that terse, pithy statements stick. We are often too verbose, and thus, less memorable. As parents, it should be our desire to make what we say memorable. This was Solomon's concern. He took profound truth and reduced it to easily understandable phrases. He used comparisons, similes, and word pictures ("apples of gold in pictures of silver"). Why? He wanted his children not just to hear but also to understand, apply, and remember! The wise parent of our day does the same.

Good parents do not constantly nag or rant and rave. They are not like a saw that rasps continually against the grain. Rather, they use words to draw pictures, to gain attention, and to stick truth in the hearts of their children.

Which of the following is easier to remember and understand?
- "Good enough is never good enough."
- "Son, don't be mediocre. You need to always do your very best."

Good parents use proverbs to help their children remember important truths. They become guideposts or beacons that point the way years after they have left their parents.

Learn to be pithy, precise, and picturesque in your correction. Wise parents do! Ask God to give you the creativity to make your parental instruction understandable, practical, and memorable.

Final thought: Use your words to grab your children's attention and focus it on God.

Day 2

PROVERBS 1:2

"To know wisdom and instruction; to perceive the words of understanding."

Knowledge vs. Wisdom

Parents impart knowledge. Good parents impart wisdom. It is good for children to know 2+2=4. It is better that they know that behind the strict mathematical code is a God of order, organization, detail, and exactness. It may be good that our children play sports, but it is far better that they see the LORD behind every event in their lives.

What is wisdom? Some have said it is the practical application of knowledge, but I don't think that definition goes far enough. James 3:15–17 describes two kinds of wisdom: earthly wisdom and wisdom from above. Earthly wisdom may be the practical application of knowledge, but people go to hell if they only have earthly wisdom. A builder may use mathematical measurements to wisely build a house. But that doesn't mean he is wise!

Fathers may think they succeed if they teach their boy a skill. Moms may think they succeed if they teach their daughters to keep house. But heavenly wisdom is more than the practice of knowledge. This wisdom is "from above." That is, it finds its home in the Godhead. Colossians tells us that in Christ "are hid all the treasures of wisdom and knowledge" (Col. 2:3). In Colossians 1:9–10, Paul prays that we would be filled "in all wisdom and spiritual understanding…in the knowledge of God."

True wisdom is not teaching our children how to behave in public, to cook, to play ball, to drive a car, or even to be a responsible adult! True wisdom is teaching our children to know and love the Lord. The wise parent points to God in daily conversation with their children: in disappointments, in stories of God's providence in their life, in how God answered prayer in Dad's job, by reminding them that God made the moon, or by remarking that God painted a beautiful sunset.

When we are so God conscious that we reveal the LORD in every circumstance of our children's lives, then we are imparting wisdom.

Final thought: Are we just parents, or are we wise parents?

Day 3

PROVERBS 1:3

"To receive the instruction of wisdom, justice, and judgment, and equity."

Great Parenting Goals 1

Here are four great personal goals for a wise parent: wisdom, justice, judgment, and equity. Today we will discuss the first goal.

We must not merely instruct in wisdom, we must ourselves receive the instruction of wisdom. *Receive* is the King James translation of a Hebrew word that means "to accept, to believe, or to commit to." The concept of possession is inherent in the meaning of this word. Thus, a wise parent must be personally saturated with wisdom. Wise parents are literally dripping with the knowledge of God in their daily lives. Wise parents are totally committed to knowing, loving, and enjoying the Lord. Is this your goal? Do you daily seek fellowship with Him? Does your heart pant for God (Ps. 42:1)?

Proverbs 1:2–4 describes the wise parent. A wise parent knows the Lord (experiential fellowship, vs. 2) and is possessed by this knowledge (v. 3). Like Paul, the wise parent counts all things but loss "for the excellency of the knowledge of Christ Jesus my Lord." Ask God to give you a thirst for Him that can only be satisfied (as David puts it) when "I remember thee upon my bed, and meditate on thee in the night watches" (Ps. 63:5–6). When this is your quest, your pursuit, and the longing of your soul, your family will soon take note! Be a receptive (possessed) parent today.

Final thought: The wise parent knows God and desires to share that relationship with his family.

Day 4

PROVERBS 1:3

"To receive the instruction of wisdom, justice, and judgment, and equity."

Great Parenting Goals 2

Here are the four goals of wise parents: to be possessed by wisdom, justice, judgment, and equity. Today we look at the second of these goals.

We must be possessed by justice. *Justice* is the Hebrew word most often translated "righteousness" and refers not to the quality of righteousness but to right living. Experiential knowledge of God leads to righteous living.

Parents sometimes mistakenly demand righteousness from their children. True biblical righteousness, however, comes from the inside. As we know and love God, our lives ooze with His righteousness. Personal, intimate fellowship with the Lord produces an inner pressure that forces righteous living into our lives. The same goes for our children.

We can force our children to do right, but this does not build righteousness in their hearts! Rules, standards, and regulations may produce correct outward behavior, but it does not change hearts.

Your mission is to instill a passion for God that works out righteousness in your children. Righteousness is not mandated or molded, it is pressed out from within! Be on guard against externally molding your children to do right. Rather, ask God to help you exude such a love for Him that your children are caught up in the same love. You will soon see the "oozing" of righteousness in their lives.

Final thought: Remember that true righteousness must always grow from the inside out.

Day 5

PROVERBS 1:3

"To receive the instruction of wisdom, justice, and judgment, and equity."

Great Parenting Goals 3 & 4

Previously we have discussed two of the four goals that Christian parents should have for their own lives. Today we see the final two goals: to be possessed by judgment and equity.

Godly parents are possessed by good judgment. The Hebrew here for the word *judgment* refers to decision-making. Its biblical usage is especially applied to leaders. Wise parents make wise decisions. But where do they get that wisdom? When our knowledge and love of the Lord possesses our souls, we make wise decisions. When our decisions are based on biblical teaching, we make wise decisions. Salvation alone does not guarantee wise choices. Only knowledge of God guarantees such.

Godly parents are possessed by *equity*. The Hebrew word for equity is an interesting one. It simply means "ease, level, or smooth." It gradually came to stand for the easy-going spirit of a person that causes them to be at peace with those around them. *Level* carries the concept of honesty and trustworthiness. These two ideas convey equity. The parent, possessed by equity, is at peace with his/her mate and children. Peace and love dominate the house rather than strife. One who enjoys God enjoys his children. One who is at peace with God is at peace with her family. The home becomes a haven for the children.

Do your children love to be around you? Are they happy at home, or does the atmosphere at home cause them to prefer being somewhere else? Do your children love to be around you? Do they sometimes choose to stay at home when they could be with their friends, simply because you are fun to be around?

Final thought: Ask God to give you peace with your children and to destroy any adversarial spirit you may have.

Day 6

PROVERBS 1:4
"To give subtlety to the simple, to the young man knowledge and discretion."

Goals for Instruction

Having seen the parent's goals for his own life, we come now to his goals for instruction. The object of parents is to "give subtlety…knowledge and discretion." Note the progression of verbs in Proverbs 1:2–4: to know, to perceive, to receive, and to give. First, we must have an intimate knowledge (experiential knowledge) of the Lord (true wisdom). Second, we must understand the implications of that wisdom. Third, we must be possessed by that wisdom. Finally, we must instill that same wisdom in our children.

Until we know, perceive, and are possessed by True Wisdom, we have nothing to give to our children. We can fuss and force; we can chastise and coerce. But until we know, perceive, and are saturated with God, we cannot impart wisdom to our children.

Give is a translation of the Hebrew word meaning "to practice, teach, or share." We can only share what we have experienced. We can only teach our children what we know, understand, and are possessed by. True instruction is far more than dispensing information! A parent IS the lesson! Jesus shared His life and His heart with His disciples. They became learners of Him.

Notice the recipients of this sharing: "the simple" and "the young man." The word *simple* means those who through lack of experience do not yet fully comprehend or understand. We often accuse youth of ungodliness, when, in reality, they only lack maturity. We sometimes misinterpret immaturity as rebellion. It takes patience and transparency to share with the inexperienced and the immature. Do you have the patience and honesty to share your life, your heart, and your experiences (failures and triumphs) in your daily walk? Transparency alone will give "subtlety to the inexperienced" and "knowledge and discretion" to the young.

Final thought: Make it your goal today to share one failure and one triumph in your walk with the Lord with your children.

Day 7

PROVERBS 1:5

"A wise man will hear, and will increase learning: and a man of understanding shall attain unto wise counsels."

Producing Helmsmen

This verse points us to the kind of children our homes must produce. Let's work backwards in this verse. The ultimate goal of a home is to produce children who "attain unto wise counsels." Literally, the phrase *wise counsels* can be translated "helmsman" (one who steers a ship). Thus, our homes are like naval academies producing young people capable of steering their own lives and rightly influencing the lives of others. When our children leave home, they must be equipped to steer their lives in a godly direction on an ungodly sea. They must, likewise, have a burden to help other youth avoid the rocky shoals of temptation.

Back up one phrase: "a man of understanding." Helmsmen understand their purpose. They understand that they are to live God's truth and to teach it to others. They understand that obedience to the Word is the only successful course in life. Is this true of your children? Are you consciously teaching them how to counsel themselves with the Word so they can counsel their peers biblically?

Backing up again we see that helmsmen "increase learning." This is how children become men of understanding. They have parents who don't just pass off this responsibility to Sunday school or Christian school teachers. Rather, the parents take the time to personally teach their children "thus saith the Lord." How much godly, biblical wisdom do your children get from you?

Finally, notice where this begins with the child: "A wise man will hear…" Hearing is paying attention. If your children would become helmsmen, you must focus their attention. You must direct their heart from entertainments and social functions to theology! You must bring them face-to-startling-face with the majesty and glory of God in such a way that they are jolted from apathy and drawn to His multi-faceted beauty! This is your mission. Will you accept it?

Final thought: As a godly parent, you should be developing children who will impact others for Christ.

Day 8

PROVERBS 1:7

"The fear of the Lord is the beginning of knowledge: but fools despise wisdom and instruction."

Our Main Aim

Many scholars consider this verse the theme of Proverbs. It certainly is foundational to Christian education, whether in the home or in school. Knowledge, which here is synonymous with wisdom as seen in the second half of the verse, begins with the fear of the Lord. Training in the home begins when youth fear the Lord. Why, then, do we skip the beginning and concentrate on the results? We can train all day, but we only train fools unless they fear the Lord! As a parent my first objective is to bring my children face-to-face with God. How? 1) By relating everything that happens in your family to Him; 2) by linking every TV program watched, every conversation started, every decision made, every news item heard, every problem faced in the home to an attribute of God; 3) by drawing your children's attention to how God is at work in every problem the family faces (whether at home, in the school, with friends, or on the job); 4) by drawing attention to the providence of God in everything that happens in the home; and 5) By keeping a record of answered prayer in the lives of the family throughout the year.

Children's minds must be renewed daily by focusing their attention on the presence and work of God. They must recognize His hand at work, love Him, and respect Him. This is where true biblical training begins. If this is not your first priority and the dominant factor in your home, you are training fools! Ask God to help you turn your home into a "praise lab" of His glory.

Final thought: If your children don't see the Lord in everything that happens, you are blindfolding them!

Day 9

PROVERBS 1:10
"My son, if sinners entice thee, consent thou not."

Youthful Naiveté

Solomon understood human nature. His warning reveals an understanding of two basic truths that endanger our children:

1. Sin is enticing. Man is born with a sin nature and a natural bent to evil. All children are born this way. This fascination with sin endangers them.
2. Youth are naïve. Fascination with sin is exacerbated by the naiveté of youth. When he calls them simple in verse four, he is not implying that they are dumb but that they do not have the experience to make wise judgments. Our children are not always rebellious. Sometimes they are just simple to the ways of the world.

This is a deadly combination. A four year old's fascination with a snake, coupled with his childish innocence, can prove deadly. Solomon's understanding of these two forces prompted him to write a ten-proverb warning. The verses that follow reveal how temptation works and what must be done to overcome it. A wise parent will teach the same principles to her children. What forces entice youth to sin?

1. The need to belong ("Come with us," v. 11). Every child wants to feel accepted. The longing for belonging has led many into sin when their heart was not actually rebellious. Naiveté caused their downfall.
2. The desire to possess ("We shall find all precious substance," v. 13). All men want. The danger is when we are controlled by our wants. It is not money that destroys a man, but the love of it. Warn your children of this temptation and model right priorities before them!
3. The failure to foresee. ("They lay wait for their own blood," v. 18). Youth do not see the end from the beginning. Their inexperience makes them shortsighted.

Final thought: Take a few minutes today to warn your children of these three problems—especially when they say, "I don't see anything wrong with it."

Day 10

PROVERBS 1:11–12, 14

"If they say, Come with us. Let us lay wait for blood, let us lurk privily for the innocent without cause: Let us swallow them up alive as the grave; and whole, as those that go down into the pit: Cast in thy lot among us; let us all have one purse."

The Need to Belong

Let's look more closely at those things that cause our children to give in to the enticements of sin. First there is the need to belong. These three verses make this clear. Notice the five uses of the word us in this passage. Children have a strong desire to be accepted. This is a part of nature and is not in itself rebellion. However, the forces of sin understand this drive and use it to seduce the naïve to fall in with the wrong crowd.

Consider your children. Each of them wants to feel accepted. Some are not accepted by their peers because of the way they dress, some because they are not academically sharp, some because they are not athletic, or a thousand other reasons. These children feel ostracized and are susceptible to following anyone who will show them attention. This is obvious in verse 14 when the child is willing to give his cash to this wicked crowd in order to belong.

As parents, be conscious of children (yours or others) who are on the outskirts. Make a point to draw them in and show them you love them and that they belong. Do not allow other children, brothers or sisters, to make fun of them or to leave them out. Teach your child the evils of mocking those who do not measure up. Champion those who are left out before others. Use every small victory in their lives as a platform to compliment them. Better they "throw in their lot" with godly parents than with the ungodly who will only take advantage of them for their own gain.

Final thought: Make home the "accepting place."

Day 11

"We shall find all precious substance, we shall fill our houses with spoil."

The Desire to Possess

The second force that makes youth prime candidates to follow the wrong crowd is the desire to possess. All men want to own, to possess. This longing for things is the "root of all evil" (1 Tim. 6:10). It is not possessions that destroy, but the love of them. Paul reminds us, "But they that will be rich fall into temptation and a snare, and into many foolish and hurtful lusts, which drown men in destruction and perdition" (1 Tim. 6:9).

This force drives youth, and its power often overwhelms them. I have seen children driven to stealing because they wanted shoes like all the other kids.

How can you use this principle in the home?

First, make sure you don't emphasize the importance of money, possessions, or career-mindedness in the home. Few Christian youth are pursuing Christian ministry. Why? They are following moms and dads who are following Mammon! Homes where dad is always preoccupied with making money, buying a new car, or getting a larger boat or where mom spends her time shopping to keep up with the latest styles, do little to dull covetous appetites.

Second, stress the value of sacrifice and submission. Hold up as examples those who gave up things of this world in order to serve God (e.g., Moses, Paul the Apostle, and William Borden).

Third, be an example of sacrifice yourself. Don't flaunt possessions, and don't honor those who do. Warn against the excesses of money. Teach your children the corrupting influences of money. Take on special ministries that require sacrifice and faith to accomplish.

Finally, exalt Christian ministry above all treasures. Encourage your children to seek ministry rather than money in their future.

Final thought: A parent consumed with possessions will produce children consumed with possessions.

Day 12

P R O V E R B S   1 : 1 8

"And they lay wait for their own blood; they lurk privily [hide] for their own lives."

The Importance of Insight

The sinners described in these verses had no foresight. They enticed naïve youth to follow them. Yet they walked the path of their own destruction! Youth lack the ability to see beyond today. This is a sign of immaturity, not of rebellion. Keep in mind that your best youth can be enticed to the grossest sins because of their innocence.

"Experience is the best teacher," we are told. Yet, we could avoid much heartache if we would but listen to those who have had the experience. Solomon here warns the simple to look beyond the now. So we must do with our children.

Parents, bare your hearts to your children! Be transparent. Share with them those times when you didn't listen to experience and the sadness it brought you. Show your failures. Obviously, you don't have to dredge up sins best left dead. But you can demonstrate those times when you failed to see the end from the beginning, and its consequences. Let them see that we all struggle but that this is no excuse for sin.

Teach them how to look at the end, not just the beginning. Use Moses as an example (Heb. 11:23–27). Teach them of Lot. Would he have made those same choices had he seen the end of his life? He was driven by the lust of gain; he lived for the moment. He was driven by the desire for what looked best. Yet it led to his destruction because he had to consider the future. Warn them that some may "lay wait for their own blood." Teach them Proverbs 1:24–32. Use examples (anonymously) from the lives of others you have known. Teach them to live with eternity's values in view.

Final thought: The wise parent teaches his children to see the ends of their actions.

Day 13

PROVERBS 2:1-5

"My son, if thou wilt receive my words, and hide my commandments with thee: So that thou incline thine ear unto wisdom and apply thine heart to understanding, Yea, if thou criest after knowledge, and liftest up thy voice for understanding; If thou seekest her as silver, and searchest for her as for hid treasures; Then shalt thou understand the fear of the Lord, and find the knowledge of God."

The Measure of Success

Verse 5 describes the goal of godly parenting: to produce youth who understand the fear of the Lord and find the knowledge of God. Academic scores do not measure success in your child. Though our children become doctors, lawyers, and influential citizens, we fail if they leave our home without a genuine fear of the Lord and understanding of how He works.

How do we produce God-fearing youth? Solomon presents several steps in the verses that follow. The next several days we will look at each of these more closely.

The First Step to Wisdom

First, youth must "receive my words." The search for wisdom begins by learning from someone else. That's where parents come in. You are the "someone else." Your children must receive your words. The word *receive* means "to take, to grasp, to seize, or to take away." We're not talking about paying attention. As hard as it may be to get a child to pay attention, the parent's job involves even more. We have not taught until our children seize upon the truth and make it their own.

Don't work on attention techniques. Work on getting to their heart! Paying attention is only the gate that leads to what you're really after, a possessed heart. How do we do that? We get to their heart through our heart. Children seize their mentor's passion, burden, and fire. If you're burned out or cold in your heart for both the Lord and His work, your children will have nothing to seize.

Final thought: Youth can't snatch fire from dead coals. How's your fire?

Day 14

"My son, if thou wilt receive my words, and hide my commandments with thee…"

The Second Step to Wisdom

Youth must hide the Word in their heart. Once more we see the parent's focus is the heart, not behavior! Behavior is only a tool, and the tool is not the product. We are equipping youth with the tools they need in life: we are fashioning their hearts. We must readjust our thinking in both education and the home. Education is about wisdom, not knowledge. The home is about the heart, not conformity. In school your child may memorize and give correct answers. In the home your child may submit to your demands. But both of these are external and may be accomplished without an ounce of grace in the heart.

Hide translates the Hebrew "storing up" or "saving" (as when someone places documents in a security box for safe keeping). It is our responsibility to make Christ and His Word so thrilling and valuable that youth treasure the teaching of the Word and long for fellowship with Him. When our children treasure what we teach them about the ways of God, we are beginning to educate them.

Today's youth, sadly, place little value on the things of the Lord. Why? There are many answers to this question, and many of them are found in the home! The entire entertainment industry from sports to Hollywood stars, video games, and the Internet often go unchecked at home. Parents are caught up in treasuring things that vanish, and peers are eaten up with materialism.

How do we fight these trends? We give them an example. We must treasure the Word. We must memorize it, meditate on it, and enjoy doing it. The conversation at home must focus on the Lord. We must share our enthusiasm for the Word with our children. Share with them each day what you have memorized. Take out a golden verse and handle it in such a way that your children are in awe. Soon they will share what they have received in their daily devotions. Then you are beginning to parent biblically!

Final thought: Encourage and demonstrate the importance of hiding God's Word in your heart.

Day 15

"So that thou incline thine ear unto wisdom, and apply thine heart to understanding."

The Third Step to Wisdom

Two problems confront the modern parent: truth is not always easy to understand, and children are increasingly less able to concentrate. Yet, without understanding, youth have not learned. This verse teaches that a person must "incline" his "heart to understanding." *Incline* translates the Hebrew word meaning "to stretch out, to spread out." Wisdom and spiritual understanding come by stretching out our minds to grasp truth.

Youth who cannot concentrate cannot learn. We can blame the problems on TV, rock music, or modern culture, but blame doesn't solve the problem. We must teach the mysteries of God to an increasing number of learning disabled children.

Be very careful that you don't succumb to writing off your child as ADD and resort to medicine. Often, the very youth who cannot concentrate in school can be led to have a heart for God. Peter was probably not the greatest student in Galilee High. He was probably "hyper-active," and always "mouthing off." Yet he had a heart that could be reached. Both Paul the scholar and Peter the scoundrel were greatly used of God. Why? Because God is concerned with the heart! Many who cannot stretch their minds to grasp subjective concepts have a heart that can be stretched out to wisdom. Your job is to reach their heart and to give them a thirst for the things of the Lord.

Final thought: Work on your child's heart, and the head will follow!

Day 16

PROVERBS 2:3

"Yea, if thou criest after knowledge, and liftest up thy voice for understanding."

The Fourth Step to Wisdom

Prayer should be a normal, but important, part of our home. Too often we thrust prayer to the corner. We might begin our mealtimes (those few meals that families are able to have together) with a short, perfunctory prayer. Perhaps at night we might have a quick prayer. We are better off not to pray in front of our children than to pray flippantly or as though we're rushing to get it over with so we can get to the more important things.

Yet, we do our greatest teaching when we pray in front of our family. Our children see our passion for God (or lack thereof) when we pray. They hear our heart cry (or lack thereof) when we pray. He who would be wise must know how to pray. Our children will learn how to pray when they hear us pray.

Charles Bridges, commenting on this passage, said: "Earthly wisdom is gained by study; heavenly wisdom by prayer." Remember that the Christian family is about heavenly wisdom.

Do you pray aloud each day for your children in front of them? Do they hear you call their names? Silent prayer for them is not enough. They must hear that you care. They must see you bare your heart to God on their behalf. Youth have had their lives turned around because they heard the earnest prayer of a mom or dad, or a pastor, or a teacher calling their name.

But don't pray fast or flippantly. It is not perfunctory prayer but passionate prayer that God hears and that impresses young lives! Cry for knowledge; lift up your voice to Him in a way that lets your children feel your passion.

Final thought: Today, in front of your children, ask God to give wisdom to (name your children). Ask God to give each child a hunger/passion/thirst for Him.

Day 17

PROVERBS 2:4 – 5

"If thou seekest her as silver; and searchest for her as for hid treasures; Then shalt thou understand the fear of the Lord, and find the knowledge of God."

The Fifth Step to Wisdom

Values are caught, not taught. If you value earthly things, your children will pick up on it, and your values will become their values. Parents who influence their children for God are those who internally value fellowship with the Lord above all the treasures of earth. If He is not your supreme value, neither will He be your child's greatest treasure!

How do children see your values? Values are seen in what parents most enthusiastically talk about. Values are seen in sacrifice. We will sacrifice time, effort, and money for that which we value the most.

- Children may think making good grades is more important than loving God. Why? Because their parents continually stress grades but speak little of the Lord to them.
- Children may think earthly possessions are more important than loving God. Why? Because their parents talk about things they wish they had.
- Children may think daily life is far more important than the Word. Why? Because parents rarely talk about the child's devotions (or their own) or the child's prayer life. Instead they talk about work, bills, and daily activities.
- Children may think sports are more important than loving God. Why? Because parents get far more excited at a sports event than at church. Their parents sacrifice for the child's participation in sports but seldom get excited about them studying the Word or memorizing Scripture.

What do you treasure? How often do your children see you seeking the treasures of wisdom in prayer, Bible study, Scripture memory, or personal devotions? Do your children see you searching, digging, growing, and treasuring your relationship with God? Only then will you "find the knowledge of God," and only then will your children "understand the fear of the Lord."

Final thought: Parents must treasure the Lord.

Day 18

P R O V E R B S   2 : 6

"For the Lord giveth wisdom: out of his mouth cometh knowledge and understanding."

Parents Need Wisdom

Christian parents know they need wisdom! Every day you are molding the lives and affecting the souls of precious children, the handiwork of God. We know we will stand before Him and give an account of how we affected their lives. Yet, children differ in their personalities, aptitudes, appearance, preferences, and needs, even in the same family. How can we wisely deal with each one? The "wisest man who ever lived" (Solomon) tells us how to gain such wisdom—go to the source of wisdom! "The Lord giveth wisdom: out of his mouth cometh knowledge and understanding."

Years earlier, Solomon was given the privilege of choosing a gift from God. Solomon chose wisdom, and his request was granted. Thus, Solomon passes his secret to us in this proverb. It was not Solomon who was wise but the God who gave Him wisdom. If we would have the wisdom of Solomon, we must go to the same source as Solomon.

Solomon asked for wisdom, which perhaps was the wisest thing he ever did. We need wisdom every day. Perhaps the wisest thing we will ever do is to ask God daily for the wisdom to deal with our children and every situation we will face that day.

Asking for wisdom is a humbling experience. Such prayers are an admission that we don't have all the answers and that the Lord alone is our sufficiency.

Final thought: Right now, humbly ask God for wisdom for this day, and make this a daily habit.

Day 19

PROVERBS 2:10–11

"When wisdom entereth into thine heart, and knowledge is pleasant unto thy soul; Discretion shall preserve thee, understanding shall keep thee."

The Benefit of Wisdom

Yesterday's devotional told us how to be wise. Today's verse tells us the benefit. What is the benefit of God's wisdom? Preservation. "Discretion shall preserve thee, understanding shall keep thee" (v. 11). *Preserve* and *keep* translate two Hebrew words meaning "protect" and "guard." In Proverbs 2 the writer names two evils from which the wise are protected and guarded: corrupt people (vv. 12–15) and immorality (vv.16–19).

For parents, God's wisdom protects us from giving unbiblical advice, from exercising undisciplined discipline, and from displaying an uncontrolled temper to our children.

But notice the recipient of this benefit: "When wisdom entereth into thine heart…" The blessings of verse eleven are not for those who know the wise (right) thing to do but for those who are governed by the wisdom they know! It is one thing to have wisdom yet another for wisdom to have us. We can be wise in our head but unwise in our actions. We can know what to do yet fail to practice it in the heat of a family discussion. Why? Because the wisdom we possess hasn't possessed us. Simply put, wisdom hasn't "entered into thine heart." Only those who are unconsciously controlled by God's wisdom experience its benefits.

And how does God's wisdom "enter into our hearts"? By spending much time in prayer and in meditation on the ways of God in the Word. Gradually, God's ways will become ours, and His wisdom will become the unconscious, controlling force in our home. Then we will escape the tyranny of mechanically trying to do the right thing, or the tragedy of doing the wrong thing. God's wisdom will protect us from error. We will intuitively do the right thing!

Final thought: Make sure His wisdom has "entered into thine heart." Otherwise, you are on your own.

Day 20

PROVERBS 2:10-12, 16

"When wisdom entereth into thine heart, and knowledge is pleasant unto thy soul; Discretion shall preserve thee, understanding shall keep thee: To deliver thee from the way of the evil man, from the man that speaketh froward things; To deliver thee from the strange woman, even from the stranger which flattereth with her words."

Wisdom in Protecting Our Children

Who wouldn't want to protect their children from the evils of society!? No Christian parent wants to see their child running with "evil" peers who have perverted truth ("speaketh froward things") and have warped values. No parent would want to see his child tempted to immorality.

But how do we protect them from such 21st Century realities? By isolating them? Such is not God's way. God would have us "in the world" but not "of the world." Our children will never influence others if they are isolated from them!

God's way is for children to be internally protected, not externally isolated! The verses before us teach how to protect our children. We must help them internalize God's truth in their hearts. Internalized truth leads to discretion and understanding which will preserve, keep, and deliver our children from "the way of the evil man," and from "the strange woman…which flattereth with her words."

The question is, how do we internalize truth in our children? Diligently follow the prescription in Proverbs 2:1–9:

- Teach them the Word (v. 1).
- Help them memorize the Word (v. 1).
- Apply the Word (v. 2) by showing them how Scripture relates to their life.
- Pray with them for understanding (v. 3).
- Place value on spiritual victories above material possessions (v. 4.)
- Teach them all you know of the character of God (v. 5).
- Help them to ask God for wisdom (vv. 6–8).

Then, your children will "understand righteousness, and judgment, and equity" and "every good path" (v. 9).

Final thought: Internal protection from evil is the only safe protection!

Day 21

PROVERBS 3:3

"Let not mercy and truth forsake thee: bind them about thy neck; write them upon the table of thine heart."

Balanced Christian Character

Mercy (loving-kindness) and truth describe the full-spectrum of Christian character. It is the balanced blending of these two qualities that makes the most effective Christian servant. Mercy without truth leads to compromise, and truth without mercy produces harshness. Mercy must be fortified with truth, and truth must be tempered with mercy.

The second half of the verse parallels the first: mercy must be bound about the neck (as a golden necklace beautifies a woman); truth must be written in our heart (must be learned, memorized, and practiced). Thus, the blend of mercy with truth makes us both attractive and intelligent in our dealings with our children.

God wants us to be attractive to our children. We must reveal the beauty of Christ in our dealings with them. In Psalm 119 David speaks of blessed people who attracted him to the Lord (vv. 1–3). Harsh, cold, letter-of-the-law strictness does not draw our children to the Lord. Rather, it grieves them (Matt. 23:4) and ultimately kills any desire they may have for the Lord (2 Cor. 3:6). We must ever be careful in dealing with childish disobedience and failure to preserve our child's view of a merciful, loving God.

Truth, however, must not be sacrificed for the sake of peace. Sin must be confronted with God's Word. The wise parent has so written the Word in his heart that he can skillfully and gently use it to construct his child's life.

Final thought: The Word can be a hammer to either bludgeon or build a life. If we use it without mercy, we may well destroy a child's desire for the things of God. If we use it with intelligence and mercy, we may build a life. *Lord, teach us how to mercifully use your Word to build lives for you!*

Day 22

PROVERBS 3:5

"Trust in the Lord with all your heart; and lean not unto thine own understanding."

Trusting God

It's so much easier to trust in ourselves than in God. New parents may read many books, call grandma when they are really stymied, or trust their instincts. Experienced parents may trust in their past experiences. All may simply "do their best" and hope it is right. But all of this is forbidden in this verse. The Hebrew reads: "but toward your own understanding do not lean!"

Rather, we must "Trust in the Lord with all thine heart." Charles Bridges calls this "the polar star of a child of God." This trust must be exclusive. No other confidence (no confidence in our knowledge, our skills, our instincts, or our experience) can exist in harmony with it. We are about a divine work, and we need divine help.

This trust must not only be exclusive, it must be entire: "with all thine heart." It is a "childlike, unwavering confidence in our Father's well-proved wisdom, faithfulness, and love" (Bridges). Why should we trust in anything else? What is my knowledge compared to His? What is my understanding compared to the Creator's? What is my talent compared to His power?

"And lean not unto thine own understanding." The wise parent must develop his understanding of parenting but never lean on his own understanding. To fail to develop our understanding in this age of technology and mass communication is sin, but to lean on that knowledge is a greater sin. The more we add to our knowledge and the more we develop our skills, the more God will use them as He sees fit. But the danger is that we will lean on them rather than trust God.

How do we know we are trusting God and not leaning on our instincts and experience? By the time we spend in prayer! Trust in God and distrust of self can be measured in direct proportion to the amount of time you find yourself asking God for help and guidance in fervent prayer.

Final thought: How much (or little) do you pray, and how much (or little) do you lean?

Day 23

PROVERBS 3:6

"In all thy ways acknowledge him, and he shall direct thy paths."

Knowing God

The Christian's greatest achievement is to know God! Paul declared: "That I may know him" (Phil. 3:10) as the mark toward which he pressed.

Solomon puts it similarly: "In all thy ways acknowledge him." *Acknowledge* translates the Hebrew word *yadha*. This word is first used in Genesis 3:5 where it is found twice: "For God doth know that in the day ye eat thereof, then your eyes shall be opened, and ye shall be as gods, knowing good and evil." Here are the two senses in which this word is used throughout the rest of the Bible: 1) to know in the sense of having information or facts, and 2) to know by experience. God knew the facts; Adam and Eve would know by experience. Thus, to acknowledge God is to know Him through His Word and through personal daily experience.

Know Him Through the Word

We grow in our knowledge of Him by spending much time with Him in prayer, and especially by meditation on Him in the Word. Your goal is not to study the Word of God but to study the God of the Word! Look for His character and His ways (how He operates) as you read the Word. Make two columns in a notebook and record in one the characteristics of God you observe as you read, and in the other record the way God operates (how He acted) in the passage read.

Know Him Through Experience

Further, you must come to know Him experientially in "all thy ways." That is, every day, in every situation, and in every problem, you must consciously observe Him and mark what He did. Again, keep your thoughts in a notebook, and review the notebook regularly.

Final thought: Faithfully seeking to know God will soon "direct your paths."

Day 24

PROVERBS 3:6
"In all thy ways acknowledge him, and he shall direct thy paths."

Don't Get Stressed

Knowing God brings blessings to the Christian. God here promises that He will direct the paths of those who acknowledge (know) Him. *Direct* literally means "make straight, level, smooth, or pleasant."

Wouldn't it be great if you could have a smooth and pleasant home? You can. At least it will seem smooth to you, even in the midst of problems. In fact, even the problems will become great opportunities for teaching your children the ways of God.

To acknowledge Him includes the idea of knowing how God works yourself, but it also includes acknowledging such to your children. Take every situation as an opportunity to show your children how God is at work. They may observe God waiting until the last moment to work, in order to test our faith. They may observe God preparing the family ahead of time for something they didn't know they would face. They may observe God answering prayer and healing a parent or grandparent in a life-threatening situation.

It is your task to make certain you acknowledge Him in front of your children. Take advantage of every situation to throw the spotlight on God. Soon your children will begin looking for God's hand and expecting God to reveal Himself. They will realize that the God of Abraham, Isaac, and Jacob, is also the present God of their family! Then your ways will be "smooth, level, straight, and pleasant." Even the problems will be exciting because you and your children will be waiting to see what God will do.

Final thought: To observe God in past experiences is to expect God to reveal Himself yet again in present experiences.

Day 25

PROVERBS 3:9-10

"Honor the Lord with thy substance, and with the firstfruits of all thine increase: So shall thy barns be filled with plenty, and thy presses shall burst out with new wine."

Do You Give?

Not every family has great substance or sees great increase. Yet, we are not excused from obeying this command. In fact, if we have a desire to glorify the Lord, we will count it a privilege to give Him the firstfruits of our increase and will do so to teach our children the sufficiency of our God.

The key to giving is found in the words *honor* (lit. glorify) and *firstfruits*. Giving comes from a desire to glorify the Lord and a desire to put Him first in our lives. The more we love Him, the more we want to glorify Him. And the more we want to glorify Him, the more willing we are to give.

Firstfruits remind us of another biblical principle: the first of everything belongs to God. The first day of the week is His. The eldest son was His. The first priority of our lives is His. In all things He was and is to have the preeminence. Israel gave the first portion of their income to the Lord. This became known as the firstfruits. It was a reminder to Israel that the produce that they reaped was the gift of God and that the land itself was His, and they were merely tenants upon it. Here is a great lesson our children need to learn.

We should make tithing and faith giving very much a part of our family's life. Our children should be encouraged to do their part and should learn early to sacrifice for the Lord. They should see their parents modeling such priorities.

But we will never be poorer by giving. Verse 10 promises that our barns will be filled, and our presses will burst with abundance when we honor Him with our tithe.

Final thought: Parents, if you would have a blessed home, be faithful in giving Him the firstfruits of your income and teaching your children to do the same. The lives of your children will be impacted by the fresh power in your life!

Day 26

PROVERBS 3:12

"For whom the Lord loveth, he correcteth; even as a father the son in whom he delighteth."

Delighting in Discipline

God corrects us because He loves us. A father corrects his son because he loves him. Following God's example, biblical correction is both directed and controlled by love.

We have already spoken about the need for a balance of mercy and truth in dealing with our children. This balance is seen in the word *correcteth*. There is a difference between correcting and punishing. Punishment repays a person for wrong behavior (emphasizing truth without mercy). Correction seeks to remedy the behavior rather than exacting payment (truth balanced with mercy). Parents do not punish; they correct!

However, if we are not careful, we will go in one of two extremes: we will punish rather than correct, or we will ignore the problem, neither correcting nor punishing. In either case, we fail in our God-given responsibility. Correction involves instruction and discipline, counsel and chastisement (Prov. 29:15). Too often we are long on the use of the rod but short on reproof. It is easier to ground our kids,or lose our temper with them than to biblically counsel. It takes little forethought to scold, and less to punish, and neither shows love. Discipline without counsel reveals laziness and a lack of love.

- He that loves will counsel (unless he is too lazy)
- He that loves will bear his soul with a child (unless he is too lazy)
- He that loves will spend much time in scriptural guidance (unless he is too lazy)

There is no true discipline without prayer and loving counsel, and that counsel should continue in weeks to come. If you're too busy for this, you're too busy! Correction is your highest calling. Avoid punishment.

Final thought: Don't be guilty of undisciplined discipline! Correct, don't ignore. Correct, don't punish.

Day 27

PROVERBS 3:13

"Happy is the man that findeth wisdom, and the man that getteth understanding."

Wise Counseling

Counseling comes in two flavors: wise and unwise. This verse identifies wise counseling (correction). How do we gain wisdom and understanding? We find wisdom and get understanding. *Find* implies searching. *Get* translates a Hebrew word that implies receiving a gift.

But where do we find wisdom? Proverbs 8:35 gives the answer: "For whoso findeth ME…" Wisdom is in the Lord. "The fear of the Lord is the beginning of wisdom." In Christ are "hid all the treasures of wisdom and knowledge" (Col. 2:3). Thus, the pursuit of wisdom is the pursuit of the knowledge of Christ. And where do we pursue knowledge of Christ? Colossians 2:7 gives us a clue: "Rotted and built up in him, established in the faith…" Colossians 3:16 further explains it, "Let the word of Christ dwell in you richly in all wisdom…" Thus, we gain the wisdom of Christ by searching to know Him in the Word.

It is our privilege to counsel and correct our children by pointing them to God's Word, and especially to the nature, character, attributes, and person of the Lord as revealed in His Word. Is the character of Christ much talked about in your home?

A parent's most often used phrase in counsel should be, "What would Jesus do?" Or, "What does the Bible say?" Too often we give advice without any reference to Scripture. We say, "I think," but what we think isn't important. What God's Word says is all that is important! But to give the right kind of counsel you must be wise in the Word and in the knowledge of Christ. Then you must let it dwell in you richly, affecting every thought, word, and action. A wise counselor is one who knows how to analyze every situation in light of 1) who God is and 2) what God says.

Final thought: Point your children to Scripture, not your thoughts, in every situation. Then both you and your family will be blessed, for "Happy (blessed) is the man that findeth wisdom."

Day 28

PROVERBS 3:24, 26

"When thou liest down, thou shalt not be afraid: yea, thou shalt lie down, and thy sleep shall be sweet. For the Lord shall be thy confidence, and shall keep thy foot from being taken."

Overcoming Fear

Fear in children is often a debilitating reality. They can't sleep at night. They are afraid to take risks (this can be good or bad). Darkness scares them. Often these tendencies are due to some misplaced confidence. Perhaps they feel insecure about themselves. Whatever the cause, the answer is found in Proverbs 3:19–26. The wise parent will teach this passage to his/her fear-bound child.

As you teach this passage, note the character of God, He is wise and understanding (v. 19); He has infinite knowledge (v. 20); He has all power (He founded the earth, established the heavens, caused the flood, and brings the rain). Shall not such a God keep the child?

- He is wise. He knows how to protect you.
- He is understanding. He knows how you feel.
- He is all-knowing. He knows everything going on in the house.
- He is all-present. He is in the earth, the heavens, the ocean depths, and the highest cloud. He is in this room. He is with you everywhere you go.

Further, show them that God's Word is their protector.

- It will give you life (v. 22).
- It will make you attractive (v. 22).
- It will keep you safe (v. 23).
- It will give you sleep (v. 24). Teach them to fall asleep quoting Scripture.

The Lord must be their confidence. You must help redirect their focus from self and situations to the awesome power of God and His Word.

Final thought: Perfect love casteth out fear. Give your child a love for God (based on both experiential and empirical knowledge of Him), and fear will vanish.

Day 29

PROVERBS 3:27

"Withhold not good from them to whom it is due, when it is in the power of thine hand to do it."

Praise Your God

Think of the power in your hand! As a parent you hold the mind, the heart, the soul, and the life of each child in your home. Your speech and actions will encourage or discourage his walk with God. You have an awesome obligation.

How do we impact children for the Lord? There are two thoughts in this passage. First, magnify the goodness of God. Second, honor the good in your child.

Would you agree that every child is due the knowledge of the goodness of the Lord? Is there any greater good than His goodness, glory, and majesty? If we are to see transformed lives, our children must see the goodness of the Lord. Sadly, many disciplers (parents) know only how to present the severity of God. Children grow up thinking of God as a prison guard who will "get me if I get out of line!" What goodness of God will you magnify today? Record it here:

A second thought is also confirmed in this verse. The good (godly) things in your child should be honored. "Withhold not good from them to whom it is due." This is important because you get what you honor. If you honor godliness, you will get it. Psalm 12:8 says, "The wicked walk on every side, when the vilest men are exalted." When we honor sports and academics but seldom honor devotions, prayer, and obedience to God, we produce outwardly successful but spiritually anemic youth. Parents will knock themselves out to get to every ballgame but never ask their child if they had their devotions! Parents will make certain their children do their homework, but never help them study the Bible! Isn't God due honor?

Final thought: You get what you honor. Find ways today to magnify God's goodness and to honor godly traits in your child. It's in the power of your hand to do it.

Day 30

PROVERBS 4:3-4

"For I was my father's son, tender and only beloved in the sight of my mother. He taught me also, and said unto me, Let thine heart retain my words: keep my commandments, and live."

Home Bible Curriculum

Verses 4–9 explain what Solomon was taught by his Father, David. Today we enter David's home to hear how he taught his son.

First, he was anxious for his son (vv. 5–8). "Get wisdom, get understanding…. Forsake her not, and she shall preserve thee…. Wisdom is the principle thing, therefore get wisdom: and with all thy getting get understanding. Exalt her, and she shall promote thee." The repetitive nature of this passage exposes David's concern for Solomon's spiritual development.

Second, He was more concerned for his son's heart than his head: "Let thine heart retain my words" (v. 4). He knew the words would be forgotten, but the heart would be remembered.

Finally, He made wisdom, not facts, the focus of his education (vv. 7–9). "Wisdom is the principal thing." Now you know why Solomon asked for wisdom when God offered to give him his desire.

What do we learn as parents? We learn that dads must take a responsible role in teaching their children. They must teach them, not simply send them to someone else. We learn that we must be concerned for the spiritual and godly welfare of our children, not just their physical and mental welfare. We learn that our main task is the forming of a heart, not the conforming of behavior. Finally, we learn that true biblical parenting creates a thirst for divine wisdom. That is the principal thing!

Final thought: Creating a thirst for God's wisdom is the parent's principal task.

Day 31

PROVERBS 4:7

"Wisdom is the principal thing; therefore get wisdom: and with all thy getting get understanding."

Your First Priority

What is most important in your home: enforcing obedience or instilling wisdom? What do you praise: outward conformity or godly character? According to this verse, wisdom is the principal thing, not perfunctory obedience. The Hebrew word for *principle* means "first" or "beginning." The primary purpose of your home is to instill godly wisdom in your children. Two thoughts emerge from this: 1) Parents (the educators in the home) must be wise, not just knowledgeable; 2) The children must first be wise, then they can learn. Unwise children do not learn. It will be your task to create wise children before you teach them!

Before we can instill wisdom in our children, we must "get wisdom" (see also vs. 5). If you do not know the Word and do not know how to skillfully use the Word, you are not fully equipped to be a parent, though you have knowledge in many other fields of labor!

The primary knowledge needed for parenting is the knowledge of God and His Word. Parents should work hard at learning the Word and studying the attributes and names of God. We are disciplers, instilling the wisdom of God in our children. How much time do you spend in the Word each day? Do you plunge its depths and ascend its heights?

"With all thy getting get understanding." Understanding refers to insight necessary to skillfully use wisdom in dealing with your child. All problems should be approached with Scripture. Psalm 119:24 reminds us, "Thy testimonies also are my delight and my counselors." Notice the use of the plural "counselors." Every problem has a verse, and every verse in the Bible addresses a problem. Your knowledge of the Word and insight in using it will enable you to point your children to the Scriptures in every situation.

Final thought: Be wise in Scripture and impart this wisdom to your children.

Day 32

PROVERBS 4:7

"Wisdom is the principal thing; therefore get wisdom: and with all thy getting get understanding."

Applying Wisdom in Real Life

Today, we apply yesterday's truth to your children. Since wisdom is the first prerequisite in raising children, we must insure that our children are wise, or their training will be fruitless. While their teachers impart knowledge, it is our part to make sure our children are wise.

How do we impart the principal thing to our children? We impart wisdom by relating every situation in life to the Word of God. Ask yourself how you would relate the following home situations to biblical principles.

Your child hides his poor math test score rather than having you sign it. When you discover his reluctance or deception, how do you respond? Do you patiently ask questions to reveal his thinking, or do you scold him? Do you punish him, or do you counsel him? What biblical principle(s) would you teach?

Your child has had a falling out with either a sibling or with his best friend at school. Now they cannot speak kindly to each other. What would you do?

Your child is really down because his soccer coach benched him the entire game as a result of some practices he missed early in the season. In talking, you realize that the coach probably did overreact due to frustration. What do you teach your child?

Your child is deeply grieved over the death of a grandparent or other close relative/friend. She asks you sincerely, "Why would God let my grandma die? We prayed for her, and she still died." What do you say to her?

Final thought: In everyday situations you must guide your children to use wisdom and act as God would act. Children often learn more from circumstances than curriculum.

Day 33

PROVERBS 4:8

"Exalt her, and she shall promote thee: she shall bring thee to honor, when thou dost embrace her."

Promoting Wisdom

Since wisdom is the principal thing for both child and parent, we should "exalt her" and "embrace her." But how do we exalt wisdom in the home?

1. Talk about wisdom and explain what it is. As you help your child with his homework, stress the difference in knowledge and wisdom. Explain that wisdom is the right use of the knowledge gained in the classroom. Make it clear that you are more interested in him using the knowledge wisely, than accumulating the knowledge. Those who train unwise children might be training a future enemy of mankind!

2. Show the results of wisdom. Again, Proverbs is full of promises and blessings to those who are wise. Stalin, Hitler, and Osama Bin Laden were all brilliant, educated men, but none had godly wisdom. They perverted their knowledge and used it to bring great destruction and devastation to the world and to themselves.

3. Take advantage of situations at home to teach children to practice wisdom. When a situation arises, biblically, wisely deal with it and lead the child to see why this is the right thing to do.

4. Urge your child to embrace wisdom (see today's verse).

How to Embrace Wisdom:

1. Study it, spend time with your child each day discussing what the Bible says about wisdom (3–5 minutes).

2. Meditate on it, develop a wisdom notebook for each child and give them a verse to record the wisdom they see in that verse each day.

3. Pray for it, James said we should ask for wisdom. Have your children pray for it each day.

4. Practice it, your child should see daily illustrations where you take situations and turn them into wisdom-making moments.

Final thought: Exalt and embrace wisdom!

Day 34

"Keep thy heart with all diligence; for out of it are the issues of life."

Guard Your Heart

The most important thing in the home is the parent's heart, "for out of it are the issues of life." The Hebrew actually reads, "Of all the things you guard, guard your heart!" The picture is that of a watchman on a wall looking diligently for the enemy. In Deuteronomy 6:6–7 God commands the Jewish fathers, "And these words, which I command thee this day, shall be in thine heart: And thou shalt teach them diligently unto thy children…."

How careful are you about your heart? Of all the things that concern you, your heart should be foremost. Why? The heart is the wellspring for all our motives, actions, words, and attitudes. Therefore your home will reflect your heart.

How Do We Guard or Keep Our Hearts?

1. We should daily fill our heart with the water of the Word. Psalm 1:1–3 describes the prosperous ("happy") man as one who is "planted by the rivers of water." In verse 2 he defines the planting: "But his delight is in the law of the Lord and in his law doth he meditate day and night." It is as parents plant themselves by the rivers of God's Word that they begin the process of keeping their heart.

2. We should evaluate our heart daily to see if any enemy has entered. Satan infiltrates our heart through our eyes and ears. If we protect what we see and guard what we hear, we will keep our heart.

3. We should exercise godly thoughts. Take a verse of Scripture and meditate on it each day. Take an attribute of God and meditate on it for five minutes. What is the attribute? How did Christ show it? What does it mean to my life? Can I manifest that attribute in some measure today? Conclude these thoughts by recording your thoughts and thanking God specifically for the things you have learned.

Final thought: Guard your heart so you may teach your children the way of life.

Day 35

PROVERBS 4:24

"Put away from thee a froward mouth, and perverse lips put far from thee."

Watch Your Words

Some children have been turned off to Christianity because of the insensitive words of a parent. First Thessalonians 5:14 teaches us that there are three kinds of problem youth: the rebellious, the weak, and the easily discouraged. Of these, only the rebellious are hard hearted. They have made up their minds that they don't want any part of Christianity.

There are many more that are easily discouraged. They are not rebellious, but they act like they are. How are they different? When you get them alone and question them, they say things like, "I want to live for God; I've tried, but it just doesn't work. Not for me…it doesn't work." This is the sign of the easily discouraged person who wants to do right but doesn't have the character, the inner strength, and the fortitude to do it. Perhaps he's a perfectionist and failure devastates him.

What do you do for him? He needs our encouragement, not our discouragement. Here is where words of affirmation and confirmation are far more powerful than words of condemnation. Condemning words will devastate the person with a sensitive, easily discouraged personality. Sadly, you can never please some parents.

Finally, the weak child has his problems. He is also differentiated from the rebellious by the desire to live for God. He has tried it but doesn't seem to have the strength. The Hebrew for *weak* indicates one who is "small souled." He just doesn't have the strength to stand against the world. How is he to be treated? The Scriptures say, "Support the weak." Support means to give him a person to lean on. He needs strong companions who will run with him and pull him away from the ungodly crowd.

Final thought: Much is accomplished with the tongue. You will either use your tongue to discourage, to devastate, and to drive your children to rebellion, or you can use your tongue to give them hope and faith and to snatch them from drifting into the crowd of the rebel.

Day 36

PROVERBS 4:26

"Ponder the path of thy feet, and let all thy works be established."

Taking Inventory

This verse has close ties to verse 23, "Keep thy heart with all diligence." Not only must we take inventory of our heart, we must take inventory of our steps. Paths of our feet refer not just the places we go but also the direction we are traveling. Here is a verse that applies to parent and child.

First, where do you go in a day? The places you go may be undermining all the wisdom you are teaching at home.

Second, where do your children go in a day? The friends you allow your children to have may be teaching them ways that are not established. You and your children should be concerned with the paths of their feet and with the paths of those with whom they run.

Third, in which direction are you headed? Are you growing in the Lord? Can you say that you are closer to Him today than you were six months ago? Can you say that you have a deeper passion for the Lord than last year? Are you making progress, or are you slipping backwards? Ponder the path of thy feet. If you keep going as you are now, where will you be in 10 years?

Fourth, in which direction are your children headed? Do you see them growing in the Lord? Do you see them acting more and more like Christ? Do they have a deeper passion for the Lord than they did last year? If you don't know, you are not "pondering" the path of their feet, a dangerous omission for a parent.

The last phrase challenges us to "let all thy ways be established." That is, make sure your ways, the things you do and say, are establishing character, building a stronger heart for God, and turning you and your children into stalwart champions for Christ. Are you establishing your ways and establishing the ways of your children?

Final thought: The parent who doesn't ponder the path of his child may later ponder, "Where did I go wrong?"

Day 37

P R O V E R B S   4 : 2 7
"Turn not to the right hand nor to the left: remove thy foot from evil."

Do You Practice What You Preach?

Consistency is vital for parents. The right way is the narrow way. If I turn left or right, I endanger my walk and my home. My shoes will be muddy. Grime and dirt will splatter my pants. My family will see it. My inconsistency will undermine my own teaching. My children will see the dirt on my feet and realize I have no authority to tell them to walk a straight path.

A parent's life is closely watched by his children. Are you faithful in Church? Are you faithful in devotions? Do you find yourself happily talking about the Lord with your children? Does the Lord naturally come up in almost every situation at home?

On the other hand, Proverbs says, "remove thy foot from evil." Do you lose your temper and discourage the easily discouraged or fail to support the weak? Do you practice what you preach?

We can't require our children to be faithful in church when we aren't. We can't tell them to flee worldliness when we persist in watching TV shows that undermine all we teach, or watch movies that are filled with words and ideas we would not allow our children to say or discuss in the home.

Final thought: We must practice what we preach because we preach what we practice! What we do speaks so loudly that our children can't hear what we say.

Day 38

PROVERBS 5:21

"For the ways of a man are before the eyes of the Lord, and he pondereth all his goings."

God's Evaluation

Ways translates a word that means "directions." *Goings* translates the Hebrew for "wagon tracks" (worn ruts, indicating repeated travel). *Pondereth* means "to weigh or to examine."

In summary, both a person's direction in life and the things he does repeatedly, are seen, evaluated, and examined by the Lord. Nothing in our life goes unnoticed by Him. We stand fully revealed before the eyes of the Lord.

Does it strike you that God sees and weighs everything you do? He knows the direction you are taking, whether you're drifting off course, whether you're slipping backwards, or whether you're growing closer to Him.

The writer of Proverbs uses this verse at the conclusion of a warning concerning immorality. He reminds young men that God sees all, knows all, and carefully evaluates and weighs their souls.

This should cause you to carefully face your day. God will be with you at work. He will see you at home, on the road, and at the store. He will weigh all you say. He will ponder your motives. He will evaluate how much you practice Scripture in situations that arise. He will observe the passion with which you teach your children about Him. He will observe how much you sacrifice your own wealth and energy to better advance the cause of Christ.

Parents, if God so ponders our path, should we not also ponder the path of our child? Should we not consider those "wagon tracks" (habits) in our own life and in our child's life that may be detrimental to the Lord? He is pondering them! What a sobering thought.

Final thought: Parents, someone more important than you will be in your home today and every day. What will He see? What will He write on His evaluation?

Day 39

PROVERBS 6:1-2

"My son, if thou be surety for thy friend, if thou hast stricken thy hand with a stranger, thou are snared with the words of thy mouth, thou art taken with the words of thy mouth."

The Power of Words

Words are crucial. They can heal or wound; they can edify or destroy. Wrong words are especially destructive in the home because young, impressionable minds are at stake. Although this passage has ill-spoken promises in mind (v. 1), the principle applies to many situations. We can be snared in the home with authoritarian and sarcastic speech, as well as with ill-spoken promises.

One of a parent's greatest temptations is an authoritarian spirit (and tongue). Because parents are supposed to have all the answers, they can easily develop a "know-it-all" attitude. This "I'm right, you're wrong" attitude is contrary to a Spirit-filled heart. Even when children are clearly at fault, the Bible tells us to rebuke them in love and "in a spirit of meekness" (Gal. 6:1), "considering thyself…" at the same time. We must remember that we also are sinners.

Sarcasm is another snare for parents. Ephesians 4:15 admonishes us to speak the truth in love. Yet, we often speak the truth in sarcasm or pride. Such words as *stupid*, *dumb*, and *idiot* should not be part of a parent's vocabulary. Such unloving words are like darts that pierce the heart of youth and may alter their life.

Finally, we must be careful of hasty speech, whether it is a blessing or a curse. As Jephthah made a rash promise (Judg. 11:30–31, 34–35), so parents must guard against a flash of temper in which they accuse, judge, or sentence their child before they have gotten all the facts and had time to cool down.

James reminds us, "Wherefore my beloved brethren, let every man be swift to hear, slow to speak, slow to wrath." Yet, are we not often guilty of blurting out words that we later regret? "Slow to speak" may be the fastest way to problem solving, while "hasty speech" most often is the slowest way to develop a life.

Final thought: Be s-l-o-w to speak in every family situation. Run every word through a scriptural filter. Remember: "A word fitly spoken is like apples of gold in pictures of silver."

Day 40

PROVERBS 7:1-2

"My son, keep my words, and lay up my commandments with thee. Keep my commandments, and live; and my law as the apple of thine eye."

How Important Is God's Word to You?

The word here translated *apple* is not the Winesap or the Yellow Delicious we love to eat. Rather, it is Hebrew for the "pupil" of the eye. The passage teaches that we are to keep and protect God's Word with the same intensity and sensitivity that we protect our eyes. Think about it, does anything cause a quicker hand and eye reaction than when an object flies at our eye? Our eyes are the most sensitive part of our bodies, and our natural instinct is to protect them at all costs.

Christian parents are here instructed to keep God's Word with the same sensitivity they have for their eyes. The best "apple" is the Word of God, but do we keep it? Do we lay up God's commandments in our home?

When a situation arises, do we use the written Word as the authority, or do we use our own words? When your child struggles with a subject in school, do we use Philippians 4:13 to focus them on Christ's power? When they fear an assignment or situation, do we quote verses that give them courage, or do we shame them for being afraid? When they disobey, do we show them which verses of Scripture (or biblical principle) they violated, or do we rebuke or lecture them for their misbehavior? When God answers prayer, do we show them that God's Word works?

Final thought: Perhaps the greatest thing we can teach our children is that God really does keep His Word! It is meant to be practiced, and, when practiced, it will bring blessings to our lives. But to be able to teach this truth to our children, we must first believe it. Used effectively and constantly, God's Word will keep your home strong and wise.

Day 41

P R O V E R B S   8 : 6

"Hear; for I will speak of excellent things; and the opening of my lips shall be right things."

Excellent Speech

Are you worth listening to? Think of it. Your child looks to you for the answers to life. If you fail to speak excellent things, you do them a grave disservice. Solomon here encourages his children to listen ("hear") because he speaks of excellent and right things. Only excellent and right words are worth listening to!

What is excellent speech? The word *excellent* in this passage is found 48 other times in the Old Testament, and in every other instance it refers to leaders or nobles. Thus, excellent speech is that which is noble and worthy of our submission. It is something worth listening to.

At home, excellent speech is that which is salted with the Word of God. The parent worth listening to applies Scripture in every situation throughout the day and shows the child that God's Word really is at work in their home.

Excellent speech comes from a parent who is so thoroughly saturated with the Word that he can hardly speak without quoting it. Excellent speech is not forced but is natural to a parent who spends time every day reading the Word, memorizing it, and meditating on ways to apply the Word to his child's life.

Excellent speech seizes upon every opportunity to ask, "What does the Bible say about (so and so)?" The "so and so" can be a wrong reaction to a parent's request, an argument, a derogatory action against a brother or sister, a failure to do a chore, or a wrong spirit. Dozens of opportunities occur daily to bring God's Word to bear upon the situation. If we speak apart from the Word, as good as our words may seem, our speech is not excellent and right and is thus not worth listening to.

Final thought: Only God's Word is excellent and right. Make sure your home is full of it!

Day 42

PROVERBS 8:11

"For wisdom is better than rubies; and all the things that may be desired are not to be compared to it."

Developing Values

Christian parents are in the business of values development. Romans 12:1–2 calls this "renewing the mind." The world, peer groups, TV and movies, and some teachers are guilty of instilling wrong values in children. It is the parent's job to establish a biblical value system and frame of reference in their child.

Today's society is materialistic. The most valuable things are the things that will not last—cars, houses, bank accounts, fame, and power (our text calls them "all the things that may be desired"). Children see materialism on TV and in movies; they see it practiced at school; they hear it from their peers. Thus they come to have little regard for spiritual wealth.

Yet, God's Word declares that "wisdom is better than rubies." Do your children believe this? How can you establish or protect their value system from the encroachments of the world? How can you instill biblical values in your child?

First, you must be sure your life is an example of one who values God's truth over man's riches. What do you talk about around them? Is your life one of material pursuit or pursuit after God?

Second, you must purposefully show your child why practicing God's Word is better than rubies. Do you encourage them to go into full-time Christian service? Do you apply every situation to Scripture? Do you give illustrations of those who violated God's truth and paid the consequences? Do you give examples of the blessings of following God's Word?

Final thought: Values are caught rather than taught. Your children's values will reflect on your efforts or lack thereof.

Day 43

PROVERBS 8:14
"Counsel is mine, and sound wisdom: I am understanding; I have strength."

Think Like Jesus

Most Bible scholars interpret *wisdom* in Chapter 8 as the personification of Jesus Christ. If that's the case, then Christ is saying, "Counsel is mine, and sound wisdom: I am understanding; I have strength." If this interpretation is right, then both parent and child must come to know Jesus in a deeper way than just salvation. Salvation is only the first step in obtaining true wisdom. Matthew 11:29 urges us to "Take my yoke upon you, and learn of me…." Paul's ambition was "That I may know him…" (Phil. 3:10).

How deeply do you know the Lord? Do you spend time meditating on His character, His attributes, and His ways? If you do, you will have counsel and sound wisdom, and your parenting will be transformed. Your advice will be the excellent speech we discussed a few days ago.

If you understand how Christ thinks, you will have deeper understanding in every situation. If you get to know Him, you will have strength to face every problem, discouragement, and trial in your life. Further you will find that your instruction will have greater power and force as you constantly imitate His ways and quote His words. Remember, He said, "I have strength."

Your children deserve the wisest counsel. Since Christ is Wisdom, doesn't it make sense that the more intimately we know and fellowship with Him, the wiser will be our counsel to our children?

Final thought: "What would Jesus do" is more than a slogan. It is a principle that must govern our daily actions. But to practice it, we must know Him deeply and intimately.

Day 44

PROVERBS 8:30

"Then I was by him, as one brought up with him: and I was daily his delight, rejoicing always before him."

Jesus' Delight

Proverbs 8 is a picture of Jesus personified as wisdom. The thirtieth verse is especially noteworthy. Christ here claims that during the creation of the world He was "by" and "brought up with" the Father. The words are reminiscent of John 1:1: "In the beginning was the Word and the Word was with God, and the Word was God." The phrase *brought up with* Him comes from the Hebrew meaning "a craftsman." That is, He was involved in the creation process with the Father. Further, Christ claims that during the creation of the world (vv. 27–30), He was present and delighted daily in what His Father was doing, rejoicing always in His presence.

Do we have such delight in the Lord? The phrase *daily His delight* is literally "daily delight." If Jesus delighted daily in the Father, should not we? What is your daily delight? We should make it our business to find one attribute or act of God in which we delight daily. Are there not enough divine attributes and actions to last us a lifetime?

In verse 31 Christ is seen "rejoicing in the habitable part of his earth" and in "the sons of men." Here then is how we should talk to our children about nature, by displaying and rejoicing in the creative glory of God. Do we talk about the stars, or do we talk of the glory and majesty of God in the stars? Here is how we should talk about our past life. Do we merely tell what happened, or do we teach them the providence of God in our life, showing them how God was behind everything that happened (how God saved you, how He used tragedy or a bad event to bring good to your life, etc.)? If we do not teach the glory of God in creation and in our life, we do not accurately teach our children. In Isaiah 6:3 the angels cry, "Holy, holy, holy, is the Lord of hosts: the whole earth is full of his glory." Do we see it? Do we show His glory to our children?

Final thought: What is your daily delight? Do you love teaching your children because you get to show the glory of God? Make Him your daily delight.

Day 45

PROVERBS 8:34

"Blessed is the man that heareth me, watching daily at my gates, waiting at the posts of my doors."

What Are You Waiting For?

Wisdom (Christ) continues to speak and promises to bless those who watch "daily at my gates, waiting at the posts of my doors." It is one thing to determine to daily delight in the Lord, but it is another to know how to do so. How do we watch and wait daily at His gates and doors?

First, we must hear (listen). The first step in meditation is to learn to open our eyes and ears to what God is saying. This includes full attention to what we read, but it also requires asking God to teach us. In Psalm 119:18, the psalmist begs, "Open thou mine eyes that I may behold wondrous things out of thy law." This should be our daily prayer as we open the Word.

Second, we must watch and wait. That is, we must be willing to spend time repeatedly going over the same passage until God shows us what it says and what it means. Waiting requires patience. Watching requires working over each word and phrase with diligence. Put another way, meditation requires time and toil. A cursory reading of the Word will miss the true beauty that is there. If I am to be blessed, I must be willing to take the time and make the effort to pour over the Word.

Third, we must watch and wait daily. Delighting in the Lord is not a one-time requirement. It is a daily privilege, and only those who daily practice it will learn true wisdom. Consistency in the Word brings blessing.

Finally, we must watch and wait daily at His gates and doors. One waits at a gate to see the owner come and go. Thus, the focus of our meditation is not on the Word of God but on the God of the Word! How do we do this? Each day, choose a verse or passage of Scripture and record in a notebook what you see and learn about the Lord. Don't focus on other things, just focus on Him as He comes and goes! Be a God-watcher!

Final thought: Do you want a blessed home? Practice waiting daily at His gates.

Day 46

PROVERBS 10:5

"He that gathereth in summer is a wise son: but he that sleepeth in the harvest is a son that causeth shame."

Wisdom in Harvesting

Carpe diem, seize the day, is sage advice. Harvest time doesn't last. It is only for a short season. The wise child understands this principle and "works while it is yet day." The wise parent learns that there are fleeting moments when they must both sow and reap in their child's life. The hearts of many children, like un-harvested fields, have been wasted by parents who slept through harvest moments!

Children don't always open up to parents. But there are those moments when they will listen and when they share their hearts. The wise parent is alert to those short moments and seizes them to sow or to harvest. How many such moments have been lost because Dad and Mom were too busy with life to stop and really listen to their child?

Sadly, parents rush through the dizzying whirl of life until one day they wake up and their child is graduating from school or getting engaged. Then they look back on thousands of missed opportunities and days that slipped by without so much as a thought about the passing of time. The summer is ended, harvest is passed, and the fruit is spoiled! When your children ask questions or when they try to tell you how they feel, it's harvest time, and you must not be asleep.

Jesus was a situational teacher. When he passed a field, tree, or vine, He seized the moment and used it to teach a lesson. This kind of parenting and teaching is unstructured, but it is most effective. It takes advantage of the "summer" of children's lives and harvests true understanding.

Is your life so busy, so confused, or so structured that you miss the harvest with your child? Do you turn vacations into harvest moments? Do you take time off to just hear, love, and enjoy your children? Don't sleep through the harvest!

Final thought: The parent who is preoccupied with self has little time to harvest. Summer comes in fleeting, unplanned moments in children's lives. Stay awake, get involved, and harvest.

Day 47

PROVERBS 10:11

"The mouth of a righteous man is a well of life: but violence covereth the mouth of the wicked."

Wisdom in Speech

If we could but think this way every time we get discouraged or want to quit. The mouth of the Christian parent should be a well of life to her children. Since we are indwelt by the Holy Spirit, who is "a well of water springing up into everlasting life" (John 4:14; 7:38), our speech, when controlled by Him, is holy and powerful.

Not so the parents who don't know the Lord. They proclaim at worst vain philosophies which ultimately will damn the soul, and at best they teach that wisdom which is only temporal and earthly. Often, their mouth, rather than being a well of life, erupts in a volcanic torrent of cursing and anger, spewing death and violence on their home.

But Christian parents have a special privilege. Their words can transform the lives of their children, save their souls from destruction and hell, rescue them from temptations, sooth their resentment, and instill right values in their hearts.

It is not simply our duty to provide material blessings for our children. Rather, it is our duty to give them life! Our mouth must overrun with life-giving words.

How do we speak with such power to our children? We do so by filling our own hearts with the refreshing waters of the Spirit. Not every parent speaks with such power. Sadly, many leave that to the Christian school teacher or youth pastor. However, it is those parents who daily fill their hearts with the Word of God and surrender their bodies to the Spirit, who have the greatest impact on their children. Only by prayer and the indwelling of the Word do we become a life-spring of refreshing water to our children.

Final thought: Do your words transform your child's life, or do they erupt with violence? Is your well full or empty? Is your tongue an instrument of righteousness or a weapon of destruction?

Day 48

PROVERBS 10:12
"Hatred stirreth up strifes: but love covereth all sins."

Wisdom in Dealing with Sin

Children will fail! Like their parents, they are sinners. How we deal with their sin is vital to their future. Although chastisement for sin is taught in God's Word, this verse focuses on other aspects of dealing with sin.

First, we must not aggravate sin. A parent's attitude, words, or spirit towards a child may provoke them to sin more. Paul reminds fathers to "provoke not your children to wrath" (Eph. 6:4). Parents can so lose it in dealing with their child's failures that they provoke them to greater sin. When we lose our temper, yell at our children, or jerk them around, we convey a spirit of hatred that "stirreth up (aggravates) strifes." Rather than help them, we drive them further from the Lord. This is a sure sign that we hate our children!

Other reactions that stir up sin include cursing, accusing, criticizing, or acting as though we are shocked that our child could do such a thing. Even worse, perhaps, is to compare them to another child or to indicate they have embarrassed you or hurt your reputation. Paul admonishes us to restore those who sin with a spirit of meekness, and that includes our own children (Gal. 6:1).

If we truly love our children, we will cover their sin. That does not mean that we ignore it or hide it from others so as to avoid embarrassment. Rather, the Hebrew word means "to cover with something else." When we help children overcome their sins, we cover them. *Cover* in this context refers to restoration. We cover sin when we take God's Word and show them how to conquer the sin, whether it is dishonesty, a critical spirit, a gossiping tongue, laziness, immorality, laziness, procrastination, or any one of a thousand other sins.

Final thought: Do you hate or love your children? The answer is seen in how you respond to their sin…and how they respond to you!

Day 49

"Wise men lay up knowledge: but the mouth of the foolish is near destruction."

Wisdom in Devotions

Wise men store up knowledge for future use. We have seen this truth before in Proverbs. Proverbs 2:1, 7 and 7:1 each admonish the wise man to hide or lay up God's Word. Here again the wisest man who ever lived advises us to lay up or store knowledge.

What does this mean in practical terms? It means more than to have devotions or to memorize verses. A storehouse is most useful when it is organized. So, the storehouse of God's Word is most useful when each verse is stored for a particular purpose. Parents face many situations as their children mature: fear, immaturity, rebellion, apathy, peer pressure, the desire to be independent, and struggles with temptation. Likewise, parents face their own problems, frustrations, imperfect knowledge, discouragements, and temptations.

How do we handle them? We show wisdom when we store up specific verses for specific needs. Parents must develop an arsenal of weapons for each sin and temptation. They must fill a treasure house with specific divine promises from which they can draw in difficult situations. They must stock up a "courthouse" of principles which will guide them in decision making.

As you read the Word each day, keep three notebooks handy: an Arsenal, a Treasury, and a Courthouse. Each time you read a verse that deals with a particular sin, write the reference and verse in the Arsenal, and note in the margin the sin it attacks. Each time you find a promise, write it in the Treasury and note the situation where this promise would help. Each time you find a principle that would help in making right choices, record it in the Courthouse with an explanation of its use. Memorize the verses; meditate on them. Spend much time in your Arsenal, Treasury, and Courthouse.

Final thought: Rich parents both store and organize God's Word to effectively use it with their children. Poor parents think this is unnecessary. Does your counseling come from God's rich storehouse or from the poverty of your mind?

Day 50

PROVERBS 10:19

"In the multitude of words there wanteth not sin: but he that refraineth his lips is wise."

Wisdom in Holding Our Tongue

There are numerous references to the tongue in this chapter with each one approaching it from a slightly different perspective. Proverbs 10:19 considers the value of holding our tongue (or the sin of speaking too much).

The more we speak, the greater the chance of sin! We are sinners, and we show it quickest in our speech. We sometimes do this when we take up the cause of our children over their teachers. We may criticize the pastor or Sunday school teacher in front of our children. We may agree with our children when they complain about their schoolteacher. A critical parent will produce critical children. Thus, the wise parent will learn to restrain his lips.

Uncontrolled anger will cause our lips to pour forth indignation and a "multitude of words." Over the course of time these outbursts take their toll on our children. We must be advised that "in the multitude of words there wanteth not sin." Sadly, these outbursts lead to apologies, but the wounds are still there. Simple apologies do not heal the wound. And even when they do, scar tissue remains!

The wise parent will not engage in critical conversations, nor will he be part of such group discussions, for "he that refraineth his lips is wise."

Final thought: What do you talk about in front of your children? Does it encourage a passion for God, or does it encourage discontent and rebellion?

Day 51

PROVERBS 10:29

"The way of the Lord is strength to the upright: but destruction shall be to the workers of iniquity."

Wisdom in Meditation

What is the Christian parent's strength? Proverbs 10:29 answers that their strength is "the way of the Lord." If the way of the Lord is our strength, then we need to ask what is the way of the Lord?

The way of the Lord is how God operates or thinks in a given set of circumstances. Those who are married learn the way their spouse acts/reacts in certain situations. So, the way of the Lord is how the God of the universe acts in various situations.

How do we learn the way of the Lord? We learn how God thinks and acts by observing Him. As we read the Word, we need to look for the ways God acts. Here is the secret to life-transforming meditation. As we read the Word, we focus on God in the story. What is the situation? How did God respond? How did God think? As we do so, we discover what makes God happy, what displeases Him, what He will do in a given circumstance. Discovering these truths will give us wisdom in how we should respond in similar situations. Observing God's ways will increase our faith as we see His care, provision, and power in the trials of life. Noting the way God operates will help us make wise decisions.

Want to keep another journal? Besides your Arsenal, Treasury, and Courthouse, you need a Ways of God journal. This may be the most important one of all. What better exercise for a parent than to spend time lovingly observing the infinite, matchless ways of God.

Final thought: Don't study the Word; study the God of the Word. No exercise is wiser. No exercise will make you stronger. No exercise will serve your children better.

Day 52

PROVERBS 11:5

"The righteousness of the perfect shall direct his way: but the wicked shall fall by his own wickedness."

Wisdom in Character

Christian parents sometimes emphasize outward ability over inward character. However, character is an infinitely better thing than talent or genius, but it is of corresponding rarity. Yet, it is character ("the righteousness of the perfect") that shall direct our way.

What exactly is this thing called character? Bishop Butler, two centuries ago, wrote that character is "those principles from which a man acts, when they become fixed and habitual in him." Our character is composed of those thoughts and actions that have become a permanent part of who we are.

Fortified with this information, look back at our verse. "The righteousness of the perfect shall direct his way…" That is, character will direct or determine the way we act. Thus, we see a circle. We begin with meditation on the immaculate character of Christ. This is the heart of "putting on the new man." Then, we seek through grace to imitate His character in our life. These acts of meditation and imitation consistently practiced become habits, which in turn, become character. In this way, we develop the mind of Christ, and thus His righteousness will direct our ways. This is the wisdom of character.

Final thought: What directs your way? Are you controlled by your own selfish flesh, by the expectations of others, or by the inward character of Christ in your life?

Day 53

PROVERBS 11:5

"The righteousness of the perfect shall direct his way: but the wicked shall fall by his own wickedness."

Wisdom in Character Development

The same verse that applies to the parent also applies to the child. Our children are developing patterns and habits that will shape their character and will guide them the rest of their lives. These habits and patterns may be righteous or unrighteous. Laziness and sloppiness both begin with bad actions that become habits. Irresponsibility and inattentiveness start with actions that lead to habits that finally become character.

What can a parent do? It is not enough to scold or punish them for disobedience. We must break the chain of action. First, we must show them the righteousness (character) of Christ. What is Jesus like? How would He act? These are questions we must constantly put before our children.

Initially, we must lead them to repeatedly take right actions in order to develop right habits in their life. They must first learn to do right because it's what Christ would do. As they mature, they will begin to do right because of their relationship with God.

Is this easy? No. It's hard. But it is accomplished with small steps. "For precept must be upon precept, precept upon precept; line upon line, line upon line; here a little, and there a little" (Isa. 28:10). Begin with a list of Christ's qualities and work on them with your children: kindness, gentleness, consistency, obedience, serving others, meditation, prayer, and putting others first.

The first habit you need to help your children develop is the habit of prayer and meditation. You should plan a time every day when they practice these exercises. Practiced often enough, devotions will become a habit. Later, this will be part of their character.

Final thought: We make our children practice their music, their sports, or their multiplication tables. But how often do we make them practice prayer and meditation? Yet, which is most necessary in life?

Day 54

PROVERBS 11:11

"By the blessing of the upright the city is exalted: but it is overthrown by the mouth of the wicked."

Wisdom in Words

Nothing is as powerful as the tongue. Here it is compared to great armies. An army may spend months besieging a city, only to have the siege fail. Yet a single word from a wicked man may bring that same city to its knees. Likewise, blessing the just and honorable citizens of a city will do more for its establishment than great battlements and walls. Thus, the tongue may be used to build up or to tear down. We must insure that our tongue is used for the former.

Here we see the power of praise. A word of encouragement may be the turning point in a child's life. Simple compliments like, "You have a talent for writing," or "You are a very thoughtful person," may do more for that child than all the scolding or admonishing of a lifetime!

How do we turn our home into an "exalted city"? We do so by blessing our children and by teaching them how to bless their friends. Sadly, we learn much more quickly how to tear people down than to bless them! Your home must become a city of praise where all the citizens love and care for each other.

Parents must guard against destructive speech. Criticism, harping on a child's weakness, and derogatory remarks should be eliminated in our homes. Children should not be allowed to criticize their siblings or friends. Use this verse or similar verses in teaching this lesson. "What does the Bible say?" should be the first words from our mouth when destructive speech is heard. Soon, the act of praising will become a normal part of your family.

Final thought: Turn your home into an exalted city by modeling praise before your children and by teaching them how to praise others.

Day 55

PROVERBS 11:12

"He that is void of wisdom despiseth his neighbor: but a man of understanding holdeth his peace."

Knowing Your Children

Why does a person despise his neighbor? He lacks wisdom or understanding of his neighbor. Lack of knowledge about another often leads to unwise and unjust criticism.

A wise parent knows her children. She doesn't just know their names; she knows them. She knows their strengths and weaknesses, she knows their likes and dislikes, and she knows their capabilities and those areas in which they struggle. This knowledge causes her to refrain from criticism or unrealistic expectations.

The unwise parent may know these facts, but she doesn't take them into account when dealing with her child. Though we may only despise the weakness of our child, the child may think we despise him. Thus, "he that is void of wisdom despiseth his neighbor…" (at least in the eyes of the neighbor).

How well do you take into consideration the strengths and weaknesses of your children—their mental capacity, their social skills, their physical needs? Do you know their hot buttons—that which will encourage them to give 100%? Do you relate to their interests (sports, cars, art, music, etc.) and encourage them in them, or is praise and acceptance difficult for you to express? Are you full of praise, or are you seldom satisfied with what they do? Do you seek to understand why they struggle in certain areas, why they don't want to talk, or why they lose their temper? Are you sensitive to their needs, weaknesses, and struggles?

Final thought: It's easy to criticize problem children, but the wise parent will take the time to get to know and understand why they behave as they do.

Day 56

PROVERBS 11:14

"Where no counsel is, the people fall: but in the multitude of counselors there is safety."

Wisdom in Counsel

Parents don't know everything! As wise as they are, they still need help. Proverbs reminds us on several occasions to seek counsel before we act (15:22; 20:18; 24:6). Although too much advice can hinder the planning process, more advice is usually better than less. Here is another evidence that humility is part of true wisdom. Those who don't seek advice think they are wise, while the truly wise seek advice from "as wide a circle as practical" (Complete Biblical Library). If we don't seek advice, we are warned that those we lead will fall. But where should we go for counsel?

First, a Christian parent should seek counsel from the Lord. David cried, "I will bless the Lord, who hath given me counsel" (Ps. 16:7). This implies prayer and seeking God's face. Prayer is yet another sign of true humility. The more I realize my own insufficiency, the more I pray. The more self-sufficient I feel, the less I pray. God, through the Holy Spirit, stands ready to give us divine insight if we will ask.

Second, we must turn to the Word. Psalm 119:24 declares, "Thy testimonies are also my delight and my counselors." You will note that "counselors" is plural. God's Word is filled with counselors. Every verse is a counselor for a particular problem. Here again we see the need of filling our Arsenal, Treasury, Courthouse, and Ways of God notebooks with godly counsel.

Finally, we should seek counsel from godly peers. Don't imitate King Ahaziah who sought the counsel of the advisors of Ahab (Israel's most wicked king), "to his destruction" (2 Chron. 22:4). It is not shameful to seek counsel from a godly pastor or a godly couple who have reared godly children. Rather, it is a sign of wisdom.

Final thought: The wise-in-heart are humble-in-heart. They seek the face of the Lord through prayer, meditation, and time in the Word before they set upon any action.

Day 57

PROVERBS 11:17

"The merciful man doeth good to his own soul: but he that is cruel troubleth his own flesh."

Wisdom in Showing Mercy

Mercy is the flip side of grace. In grace I get what I don't deserve. In mercy I don't get what I do deserve. Biblical mercy is a divine enablement. It is a fruit of the Spirit. This mercy is not showing pity in words or in looks, rather it is showing kindness and love from the depths of our heart when a child misbehaves. Mercy does not avoid chastening, but when the chastening is done, mercy continues to show kindness and love toward the one chastened. (Mercy is not just an attitude but also an action of loving-kindness toward the offender.) God chastens believers for their sin, but in His mercy He continues to love and care for us, offers full forgiveness, and continues to shower us with blessings.

Christian parents must faithfully chasten their children, but they must be careful not to cruelly punish them! Our chastening must be done in love and compassion. Too often we err in either not punishing our children or in punishing them too severely! Both are wrong. This verse seems to address those who chasten too severely. It may be called "undisciplined discipline." Throwing things, screaming, slapping our children, or physically shoving them will only cause bitterness and resentment. Ultimately harsh punishment will come back to trouble the flesh of the undisciplined parent!

Final thought: Proverbs reminds us that those who are merciful do good to their own souls. Charles Bridges reminds us, "The merciful man will always find a merciful God (Ps. 41:1)."

Day 58

PROVERBS 11:22

"As a jewel of gold in a swine's snout, so is a fair woman which is without discretion."

Wisdom in a Pig's Snout

Character is everything! Youth do not know this. Their emphasis is on the outward appearance, clothes, hairstyles, possessions, looks, and athletic ability. Yet, these are but vain things that fade with the years.

It is our job to impart this wisdom to our children. But do we know how? First, we should give them biblical examples.

- Saul was outwardly impressive, but he lacked character and ended his life in disgrace. He was a gold jewel in a pig's snout.
- Paul was nearly blind, was not an orator, but had great character and God used him mightily.
- Lot had possessions but no character.
- Abraham had possessions and character.
- Moses turned his back on wealth but had great character.
- Daniel was a captive, but his character advanced him to second in the kingdom.

Next, we must take advantage of situations that arise in our home to teach proper values to our children. Each month, have your child prayerfully work on a different part of the fruit of the Spirit. Define it, have them find verses of Scripture about it, and as situations arise ask: "Is that the way we show love (or whichever part of the fruit you are exploring)? What could you have done instead of what you did? How should you have responded? Why?" Honor your child when he demonstrates character over appearance during the month.

Final thought: Your goal is not to bejewel pig snouts but to change snouts into something beautiful!

Day 59

PROVERBS 11.29

"He that troubleth his own house shall inherit the wind: and the fool shall be servant to the wise of heart."

Wisdom in Godly Unity

A house must be at unity with itself, with father, mother, and children all committed to Christ and living by biblical principles. Such a home is blessed by God (Ps. 133). Often, however, (as Charles Bridges puts it), "the unspiritual, or ungoverned passion of the father in the home blights the comfort of the family. In deed a parent cannot neglect his own soul without injury to his family."

Prayerless, careless parents bring a curse instead of a blessing upon their home. A father deprives his family of blessings when he is unsaved, or knows not the power of prayer, or sets an ungodly example for his children. Instead of enjoying God's blessing, he "inherits the wind," and his family is impoverished. It was this way with the rebellion of Korah (Num. 16:32–33), the sin of Achan (Josh. 7:24–25), and the neglect of Eli (1 Sam. 2:32–33).

Whether a parent or a child, we trouble our family when we don't pray, when we are unfaithful in church, or when we are governed by human reason and the impulses of the flesh. The cursing, drunken, arrogant father brings his house to ruin. The father who is too busy to spend quality time with his children shall ultimately find himself impoverished as his children go astray. The self-righteous, know-it-all dad is actually the fool who will ultimately serve "the wise of heart" while his house is blown by the winds of ruin.

Final thought: A wise father makes spiritual and godly unity his goal in the training of his children and in the leading of his wife.

Day 60

"A prudent man concealeth knowledge: but the heart of fools proclaimeth foolishness."

Wisdom in Discernment

There is a time to teach our children, and a time to refrain from teaching them. Charles Bridges says, "Every truth is not therefore fitting for every person or for every time." God revealed His Word gradually. While Christ was on earth, He on occasion charged his disciples "that they should tell no man that he was Jesus the Christ" (Matt. 16:20). Later he told them, "I have many things to say unto you, but ye cannot bear them now" (John 16:12). Christ often spoke in parables to the public but explained the meaning when he was alone with the disciples. David declared that he spoke to those "that fear God" (Ps. 66:16).

This truth must be remembered in dealing with youth. There are truths that are meaningless to a child until he is saved. Ungodly men who had been taught Christian doctrine have started most cults. What does this mean for a parent? First, we must make certain our children know the Lord. Then, we must carefully explain truth as they are capable of hearing and accepting it. To force truth on those who refuse to accept it is to feed pearls to swine and will inevitably produce a rebellious child who is hardened against the things of God.

Preaching standards and forcing outward holiness on the unregenerate and rebellious child will only embitter him toward God. Children must be led, not driven, to accept truth and holiness. At the first signs of rejection, they should be taken no further. Rather, their rejection of truth should be tenderly, patiently, and carefully weeded out. When they come to accept that truth, they may be further informed. Thus, they are taught line upon line, precept upon precept as they accept the lines and precepts.

Final thought: Parents must be discerning and sensitive to the spiritual limits of their children. They must never seek to take them beyond their spiritual receptivity.

Day 61

PROVERBS 12:25

"Heaviness in the heart of man maketh it stoop: but a good word maketh it glad."

Wisdom in Encouragement

I t is the Christian's privilege to encourage rather than discourage. Joseph encouraged his brothers by speaking kindly to them in spite of their treatment of him (Gen. 50:21). Moses encouraged Israel at the Red Sea (Exo. 14:13). The Lord encouraged Israel (while warning of their imminent captivity) with these wonderful words: "For I the Lord God will hold thy right hand, saying unto thee, Fear not; I will help thee" (Isa. 41:13).

Christ Himself set an example of encouragement. We find encouragement on His lips as he healed the man sick of the palsy (Matt. 9:2), as He walked on the water before his frightened disciples (Matt. 14:27), and when he told the disciples that even the hairs on their heads were numbered (Matt. 10:30).

The Holy Spirit is called the *Paraklete* meaning "to encourage, to comfort, or to console." Thus, when we are filled with the Spirit, we will encourage our children. In 1 Thessalonians 5:14, Paul admonishes us to "warn them that are unruly (rebellious), comfort (encourage) the feebleminded (easily discouraged), support the weak, be patient toward all."

Find ways to encourage your children. Praise them for small victories; teach them the promises of God (Phil. 4:13; Isa. 41:13; 1 Thess. 5:24); comfort them when they fail. Challenge them with examples of underdogs who won (Moses–speech impediment, David—lowly shepherd, Amos—fruit-picker, Peter—uneducated fisherman, and Matthew—hated tax-collector).

Final thought: Good words make a glad home ("a good word maketh it glad")! Are your children encouraged or discouraged when they come home? Remember: Satan discourages, while God encourages.

Day 62

PROVERBS 13:4

"The soul of the sluggard desireth, and hath nothing: but the soul of the diligent shall be made fat."

Wisdom in Dreams and Diligence

It's good to be a dreamer; it's better to be a doer! Nothing is accomplished without a dream, but dreams don't make it happen. There are those who desire to grow spiritually; they want to have power with God. However, such power cannot be purchased; it must be earned. There is no other way to learn the Word apart from study. Here is a principle children must learn. It is not the dreaming but the doing that matters.

We live in an age of shortcuts. We have instant potatoes, instant coffee, instant tea, and instant gratification. We can go to the internet and find whatever we need instantly. Thus, we want quick solutions to character and godliness! Adam thought that by simply eating a piece of fruit he would be godly! What a concept—instant godliness! But it didn't work. There are no shortcuts to godliness, character, or success. God told Joshua that good success would come if he would meditate in the Word day and night (Josh. 1:8). That implies work, consistency, sweat, and perseverance. Today's youth must be taught the value of sweat-equity. Character and godliness do not come by chance, or by dreaming, but by diligent effort.

Don't make life easier for your children! Lamentations 3:27 reminds us, "It is good for a man that he bear the yoke in his youth." Children need to learn the lessons of sweat! Soft pillows don't make strong men. If things come easy for your child, find ways to make them more difficult! Always keep the carrot just a little beyond the horse's nose so that he is always stretching, for by stretching, and straining, and sweating, we grow.

Final thought: Stretch your children!

Day 63

PROVERBS 13:7

"There is that maketh himself rich, yet hath nothing: there is that maketh himself poor, yet hath great riches."

Wisdom in Priorities

What is your goal in life? Is it to advance in your job so that you can make more money and enjoy the pleasures of this world? There are those who work for wealth yet are miserable. They have the houses, cars, and possessions, but in gaining these they have lost their families and true happiness. Fathers, pursuing their fortune, have lost their sons and daughters. Parents, seeking to increase their wealth, have found themselves spiritually bankrupt, divorced, or broken in health. They make themselves rich yet they have nothing.

However, godly parents who invest their lives in their children may make themselves poor yet have great riches. They count as their wealth godly children who will one day serve the Lord as preachers, teachers, Christian businessmen, and leaders in their church. Rather than "inherit the wind," they enjoy God's blessings. It is far better to impact a life and drive an older car, than to destroy a home and drive the latest model! Take courage, parents. Invest in the lives of your children and you will have "great riches." You will have eternal, rather than temporal, results.

Hebrew scholars interpret this verse thusly, "He that pretends to be rich, shall have nothing." There are those who drive nice cars, live in beautiful homes, and wear expensive clothes and jewelry but who are failures at home. Outwardly, they pretend to have it all together, but behind the scenes there is poverty. Their children are ungodly and despise their parent's hypocrisy. Their spouse has little respect for them and simply waits for the children to be gone so he or she can leave as well. How much better to have little in this world, but be rich in God!

Final thought: True wealth is measured in lives saved, not in dollars saved! In what are you investing?

Day 64

PROVERBS 13:10

"Only by pride cometh contention: but with the well advised is wisdom."

Wisdom in Disagreements

If you are alive, you will have disagreements. You will not always agree with your spouse, your co-workers, your best friend, or your children. How we handle those disagreements will prove our character. When driven by pride, disagreements engender strife or contention. When driven by wisdom, disagreements lead to counsel. Bridges notes, "The desire of preeminence (3 John 9); revolt from authority (Num. 12:2); or party spirit (1 Cor. 3:3–4), all produce the same results." Thomas Scott wrote of the proud man: "Some point of honor must be maintained; some insult must be resented; some rival must be crushed…; some renowned character emulated; or some superior equaled and surpassed." All these attitudes cause disunity in our families.

The proud man thinks himself wise enough. He asks no counsel and thereby proves his lack of wisdom! But the wise man knows that he needs the counsel of wise men!

The wise man will also allow himself to be misjudged or misunderstood rather than stir up strife. Philippians 2:3 admonishes us: "Let nothing be done through strife or vain glory; but in lowliness of mind let each esteem others better than themselves."

When you disagree, seek counsel from God, from His Word, from wiser men, and from the one with whom you do not agree. Often the disagreement is over some misunderstanding or misinformation.

Final thought: It's natural to disagree. It's sin to contend!

Day 65

PROVERBS 13:16

"Every prudent man dealeth with knowledge: but a fool layeth open his folly."

Wisdom in Responding to Disobedience

Those who think before they act are wise. Those who don't think reveal their foolishness. This axiom may be applied to how parents respond to their child's misbehavior or disobedience.

Do you tend to immediately reprimand your child, or do you get the facts before you act? We may see something we think is wrong and immediately respond by rebuking or admonishing our child, only to find that things were not as they seemed. In doing so, we reveal ("layeth open") our folly!

Better that we approach all apparent misbehavior or disobedience by first asking questions. "John, what did you say?" "Susan, what did you do?" "Why did you do that?" "What did you mean?" "Is this what I am hearing you say…" (then repeat what you think they meant)?

Let's say two friends have a flat tire and miss curfew. They get to their respective homes an hour late. One father meets his son at the door, immediately blows his top, asks for the keys, and grounds him for six months. The other father calmly asks where they were and why they were late. He expresses his concern because he loves his son.

Which father is right? What was foolish about the first father's reaction? The circumstances were not considered. The foolish father treated the breaking of a rule as though it were rebellion, thereby damaging his integrity and wounding his son. He acted without knowledge. The second father avoided "laying open his folly," and "provoking" his son "to wrath" (Eph. 6:4). In doing so, he preserved his own integrity and that of his son.

Final thought: Get the facts before you react! Display wisdom, not folly.

Day 66

"He that walketh with wise men shall be wise: but a companion of fools shall be destroyed."

Wisdom in Companions

The obvious application of this verse is to walk with wise men, but let's take the application further. Who is wiser than God? Since God is all-wise, we would be wise to walk with Him!

In Genesis 18:17–19, God reveals His friendship with Abraham. Because of this, God determined to tell Abraham His plans to judge Sodom and Gomorrah. God asks, "Shall I hide from Abraham that thing which I do?" Why is there such intimacy with Abraham? Abraham walked with God. Matthew Henry suggests: "He was a friend and a favorite… [and] the secret of the Lord is with those that fear him (Ps. 25:14; Prov. 3:32)." He adds: "Those who by faith live a life of communion with God cannot but know more of his mind than other people (Hosea 14:9; Ps. 107:43)."

Further, Abraham is given special insight because "…He will command his children and his household after him" (Gen. 18:19). God gives special wisdom to those who both walk with Him and are committed to teach the next generation the secrets of the Lord! As parents we have two thrilling privileges: 1) to become an intimate companion of God and 2) to teach our children the secret things He teaches us!

Final thought: We must learn to be a friend of God. We must walk with Him in intimate prayer and meditation. Then, we must learn to share our passion for our Friend with our family.

Day 67

PROVERBS 13:24

"He that spareth his rod hateth his son: but he that loveth him chasteneth him betimes."

Wisdom in Discipline

Balance is necessary in discipline. On the one hand we must be understanding parents, we must take time to get all the facts, and we must not make rushed or rash decisions. Yet on the other hand, we must discipline misbehavior. Showing mercy does not rule out discipline. If we truly love our children, we will discipline them. However, we must be certain that our discipline is disciplined!

Undisciplined discipline is as wrong as lack of discipline. If we are to discipline after a godly sort, we must keep the following in mind:

- Get all the facts before you discipline.
- Counsel your child with Scripture passages that will help him overcome his problem.
- Assure your child of your love and concern for him.
- Pray with him, and ask God to give you wisdom in giving the proper discipline.
- Administer the discipline in a prudent fashion.

He that "loveth him chasteneth him betimes." *Betimes* translates the Hebrew word meaning "early;" that is, before the disobedience becomes a habit. Parents mistakenly let their children get by with inappropriate actions until they become habits; then, too late, they try to discipline.

Final thought: Wise parents see improper actions developing and deal with them before they become habits through careful scriptural counseling and other appropriate action.

Day 68

PROVERBS 14:4

"Where no oxen are, the crib is clean: but much increase is by the strength of the ox."

Wisdom in Growth

Growth costs much. Every step forward requires a sacrifice. Solomon, writing to an agrarian culture, reminds Israel that a farmer who does not own oxen has a clean barn but no food! If he wants to eat, he will have to endure the toil of constantly cleaning a messy barn. So, take your pick, plenty to eat and a dirty barn, or a clean barn and starvation!

Charles Bridges comments, "God works by means, not by miracles. We must take good care of the farm, if we want an abundant harvest…Spiritual fields, too, where there are no laborers, remain empty."

So it is with Christian parents. If we would see clean hearts in our children, we may have to sacrifice a beautiful house or a perfect schedule. Do you focus on an immaculate home or a clean heart? Do you spend your time shepherding your career, or shepherding your child? Do you focus on your hobbies and entertainment, or are your children your hobby? If we want to impact the souls of tomorrow's leaders, we must be willing to have a dirty barn and a messy schedule!

Sometimes that barn is our house! If we go to our children's ballgames, or let them invite their friends for a sleepover, or buy those special tennis shoes they want, or make sure they are in a Christian school, we might have to let our house go! We may drive a less expensive car. We may have less time for cleaning and cooking. We may not have the best furniture. Our Saturdays may be given to playing with our children and giving the house a quick once-over. But that may be the trade-off for godly youth!

Final thought: Dirty barns are sometimes necessary for clean hearts!

Day 69

"The heart knoweth his own bitterness; and a stranger doth not intermeddle with his joy."

Wisdom in Judging Others

Every man is an island. The deepest emotions (bitterness and joy) can't be fully understood or expressed by the soul. Everyone knows himself as no one else does. No two of us are alike, and these differences of mind, character, and emotions prevent perfect understanding, even in the closest friendships.

Eli totally misjudged Hanna, and instead of comforting, he rebuked one who needed understanding (1 Sam. 1:10–14). Gehazi harshly rejected the Shunamite woman and started to push her away from the man of God through his ignorance of her bitter sorrow. Fortunately, Elisha had better insight and declared, "Let her alone; for her soul is vexed within her" (2 Kings 4:27). Job's friends misunderstood his heart and proved to be worthless physicians and sorry comforters (Job 13:4; 16:2).

Parents must be careful when they rebuke their children. They must not assume that the outward action is a true manifestation of evil or good within! Only God's Word and the Holy Spirit can adequately pierce to a person's inner needs and struggles, for only the Lord knows what is in man!

We must bring children to one point: "What does the Bible say?" Taking them to the Bible and applying specific verses to every problem or situation allows God to apply the Word to their deepest thoughts and motives.

Final thought: We don't know what our children are really thinking and feeling, but God does! Let the Word, rather than your opinion, be their help.

Day 70

PROVERBS 14:13
"Even in laughter the heart is sorrowful; and the end of that mirth is heaviness."

Wisdom in Discernment

Things are not always as they seem. A child's laughter may hide sorrow, anger, hurt, or humiliation. A self-assured bravado may cover feelings of insecurity and worthlessness. A lack of concentration in homework or school may reveal unresolved conflicts at home or elsewhere. A wise parent will get to the heart of the issue and will show the child how to biblically overcome it.

When an honor student in science could not pass his reading comprehension test, a wise teacher asked, "What was your mind doing when you were reading the story?" The student's reply revealed resentment toward a male teacher who had expelled him from a class for something he didn't do. The deep, unresolved conflict manifested itself in a lack of concentration. The wise teacher asked him what the Bible said he should do (after reading several verses on forgiveness). The student, understanding what the verses taught, responded, "Oh, no. I could never do that." Later, however, he went to the teacher and resolved the conflict. His problem was deeper than a lack of concentration. His problem was disobedience to the Word. His feelings of bitterness interfered with his concentration.

Sometimes the same is true in the home. Our children may hide deep resentment toward a parent over some misunderstanding in the past. This resentment may be hidden by forced laughter, a false bravado, lack of concentration, failure to have devotions, criticizing the "good kids" at school, clamming up, avoiding eye contact, a desire to be away from the house, or a score of other things. Wise parents will look behind the façade to discover the true heart condition.

Final thought: Your mission is to get beyond symptomatic problems. You must discover the root problem and lead your child to biblically deal with it.

Day 71

"He that is soon angry dealeth foolishly: and a man of wicked devices is hated."

Wisdom in Reactions

Derek Kidner writes, "...to see a situation calmly is to see it clearly." Here we see the sin of irascibility—acting on the state of our feelings rather than the merits of the case. It is sin to be governed by feelings. A Christian's standard is to be "filled with (controlled by) the Holy Spirit." When anything else controls us, whether it be our emotions, our peers, the flesh, or substances (alcohol, drugs), we violate Scripture. God alone must control our actions/reactions. A loose tongue and a quick temper are signs of foolishness in the heart because they are proof that God is not in control. When we scream at our children, make rash judgments, or display quick anger, we reveal that self, rather than God, controls us.

Further, quick tempers often lead to "wicked devices." Bridges puts it this way, "But sin grows from weakness to willfulness." A man who at first is "soon angry" may later become cruel and calculating in planned malice.

If you have a problem with making quick judgments, with a short temper, with over-reacting, or with yelling at your children, you have become focused on "my rights and my way" rather than on being controlled by the Lord. Surrender your mind, your emotions, and your temper to God. Fill your mind with Scripture that deals with the sin of quick judgment and the wisdom of temperance. Memorize and meditate on the following verses: Prov. 14:17, 29; 16:32; 19:11; Ps. 37:8; Eccles. 7:9; and James 1:19.

Final thought: "Be not hasty in thy spirit to be angry: for anger resteth in the bosom of fools" (Eccles. 7:9).

P R O V E R B S   1 4 : 2 6

"In the fear of the Lord is strong confidence: and his children shall have a place of refuge."

Wisdom in Confidence

What a great verse for parents! Those who fear the Lord become hiding places or places of refuge for their children. There are many blessings associated with fearing the Lord. The one highlighted by this verse is "strong confidence," or in the Hebrew: "the strength of security." Fathers who fear the Lord conduct themselves in a way that causes their children to feel safe and secure. The stability of the parents makes the home a place of refuge. The children love their home. They would rather be there than anywhere else!

Parents who fear the Lord manifest strength and security that attracts children for advice and counsel, for prayer, and for assurance. Rather than turning to others, children find their own home is a refuge from the problems of life. Children sense a wisdom that will protect them from "deadly snares" (14:27 and 13:14).

What does it mean to fear the Lord? It is to so know Him and to be so saturated with His Word that your words, your actions, and your spirit reflect Him in everything you do.

Final thought: Your relationship with the Lord should be so strong and evident that your children feel safe and secure in your counsel.

Day 73

PROVERBS 15:1
"A soft answer turneth away wrath: but grievous words stir up anger."

Wisdom in the Face of Anger

This verse, like many in Proverbs, seems too obvious to mention. The proverbs, however, are given to increase insight. What insight do we gain from this verse?

First, it is never becoming for a Christian to be angry. In fact, a Christian should be adept at deflecting anger ("turneth away wrath").

Second, anger is most often stirred or quieted with a single tool—words! Words can either turn away anger or stir up anger.

Third, we must listen carefully to those who are angry so that we can respond with soft words rather than grievous words. We should always ask ourselves, "Do I really understand why this person is upset? What words will stir up their anger, and what words will soften their anger?"

Fourth, we must be in control of our own emotions so that we can be calm in the face of wrath. Proverbs 25:28 reminds us, "He that hath no rule over his own spirit is like a city that is broken down, and without walls." Such a city, in Solomon's day, was defenseless. When we lose control of our temper, we open ourselves up to trouble!

Final thought: "Let your speech be always with grace, seasoned with salt, that ye may know how ye ought to answer every man" (Col. 4:6).

Day 74

PROVERBS 15:2

"The tongue of the wise useth knowledge aright, but the mouth of fools poureth out foolishness."

Wisdom in Using Knowledge

Knowing is not enough. We must know how to use what we know! An unwise parent may misuse knowledge to the detriment of her children, while a wise parent will use knowledge "aright."

How can knowledge be misused? Some use their knowledge to twist Scripture and give it an unintended meaning. Knowledge may puff up one's pride (1 Cor. 8:1), causing a father or mother to display an air of superiority over his children. Statements such as "because I said so" or "do you think you know more than me?" are a dead give-away of a proud or frustrated parent. Such parents may browbeat their children or show contempt for their actions or answers. Thus, "the mouth of fools poureth out foolishness."

A more common problem is to use knowledge in place of Scripture. This can be a major problem with parents. Though we know the Bible, we don't always apply it to our children's lives. How do we handle a child who suffers from fear, anxieties, pride, anger, bitterness, and so on? Do we know how to use the Scriptures, or do we take them to a psychologist? Does not God's Word tell us, "Thy testimonies also are my delight and my counselors"? If the Word of God is sufficient, then why do we use human reasoning to help our children? The purpose of parenting is not to indoctrinate them to our way of thinking but to renew their minds so as to think Christ's thoughts! We must meet children's problems head-on with scriptural principles, or we have not used knowledge "aright."

Final thought: Knowledge is a powerful tool. It can build or destroy. Ask God for wisdom to use it correctly.

Day 75

PROVERBS 15:2

"The tongue of the wise useth knowledge aright, but the mouth of fools poureth out foolishness."

Wisdom in Using Knowledge Aright

Our last devotional dealt with the wrong use of knowledge. Today we consider how to use knowledge "aright."

Right use of knowledge will creatively apply scriptural truth to children's lives. The Bible is not a fact book—it is a life book. Children may learn facts, but if they are not taught how to live those facts in real-life situations, they do not have proper knowledge. When I face fear, what do I do? How do I handle struggles at school? When other children do not accept me, what do I do? How do I handle guilt for things in my past? How do I grow in the Lord? These are questions that must be answered with the Bible. Right parenting will show your children what the Bible says about these and a thousand other internal problems they face.

Right use of knowledge will exalt God in all we teach our children. They must see the majesty of God in nature, history, current events, manual labor, and the arts, as well as in Scripture. Jesus accused the Pharisees of searching Scripture but not seeing the Lord in it (John 5:39). Children must be dazzled with the majesty of God rather than being in awe of our knowledge of the facts in the Word!

Final thought: To use knowledge aright we must analyze our child's needs, study the Word for answers, and make the Bible central and practical.

PROVERBS 15:4

"A wholesome tongue is a tree of life: but perverseness therein is a breach in the spirit."

Wisdom in Mending Broken Walls

James teaches us that the tongue can destroy or give life. Here we are told that the tongue that gives life is wholesome. The Hebrew word translated *wholesome* means "to heal" or "to restore" that which is broken or hurt. Conversely, the perverse tongue breaks the spirit of another. The language of Proverbs pictures a castle wall that has been breached in siege warfare allowing the enemy to rush in and capture the defenseless citizens. Parents must be healers and restorers building up the wall where it has been knocked down.

Often the breached spirit manifests itself in acting out or in clamming up. A healing or restorative parent looks beyond the untoward actions and words of his child and sees a spirit that needs mending.

More importantly, the restorative parent seeks to mend (heal) those broken walls with wholesome words. The following are among the healing words (wholesome words) a restorative parent will use: "God knows and cares," "God is able," "God is here," "God made you," and "God placed you in your family." A restorative parent takes time to counsel from the Bible and shows the child how to apply Bible truth to rebuild their "walls." A restorative parent asks questions rather than lectures. "What did you do/say?" "What made you say/do that?" "What should you have said/done?" "What do you think the Bible says about this?" These are but a few of the questions you should ask as you help your child rebuild the walls of his spirit.

Final thought: Learn to be a wholesome (restorative) parent!

Day 77

PROVERBS 15:17

"Better is a dinner of herbs where love is, than a stalled ox and hatred therewith."

Wisdom in Love

Two thoughts race side by side in this verse: 1) money is not the most important consideration and 2) things are not always as they seem.

In Solomon's day, ownership of an ox indicated wealth and success. Yet Solomon reminds us that there are things far more important than wealth.

Today's youth are pressured to accept a materialistic value system. Parents may unwittingly add to this pressure by showing partiality to one child who is better looking; who displays athletic, academic, or artistic skills; or who exhibits polite and cooperative behavior. Yet, appearance, ability, and even behavior may have little to do with the condition of a child's heart. (Solomon warns that those who use flattery and smooth words may, in fact, have something to hide!)

This brings us to our second thought: things are not always as they seem. Lot chose on the basis of appearance, and his choice ruined his family. That which looked great from a distance was a mirage. Two hundred yards from the Jordan the land was too saline to support vegetation! What appeared rich was, in fact, poor.

The same can be true in your child's life! Smiles may hide sadness. Laughter may cover tears. Good behavior may hide a devious heart.

Final thought: Teach your children the truth of Luke 12:15. Life does not consist of possessions. Don't equate godliness with politeness! The good citizen at home may not be a good citizen in heaven!

Day 78

PROVERBS 15:28

"The heart of the righteous studieth to answer: but the mouth of the wicked poureth out evil things."

Wisdom in Thoughtful Counsel

A quick response is often a sign of pride. When we think we know it all, we speak on impulse. When we realize we are but sinners, we don't trust our tongue.

A righteous parent does not "pour out" his thoughts. He does not snap at his children. Rather, "the righteous studieth (ponders) to answer." But what must we ponder and how? First, we must search the Scriptures asking, "What does the Bible say about this situation?" Everything we say, and the way we say it, must be in agreement with Scripture. Second, we must study the people involved (our child, our spouse, a co-worker). We must consider what they said or did and what they really meant. We must consider other situations they may face that affect their actions and reactions. Finally, a righteous parent should pray and seek God's face before answering.

Lou Priolo, commenting on this verse, writes: "It is often necessary to invest extra time, effort, and thought in selecting just the right words to express which biblical injunctions have been violated, which additional passages may be cited to support the indictment, the questions that will be asked of the child, and the manner in which the reproof will be administered."

Final thought: Think twice before you speak once! Your words can destroy more quickly than they build up!

Day 79

PROVERBS 15:30

"The light of the eyes rejoiceth the heart: and a good report maketh the bones fat."

Wisdom in Our Face, Part 1

We not only have to look at our children every day, they have to look at us! Solomon states that what they see in our faces and hear from our mouths is important. Paraphrasing this verse for parents it might read: "A bright face and good news make for a healthy home."

The Bible speaks of two aspects of the face: it's affective nature and its reflective nature.

As to its affective nature, Solomon says, "A merry heart doeth good like a medicine…" (Prov. 17:22). Your face will affect the atmosphere of your home! If you want a changed atmosphere, change your face! How? By considering the reflective nature of the face.

Reflectively, the face is a mirror of the soul. "A merry heart maketh a cheerful countenance" (Prov. 15:13). Cain's sin caused his countenance to fall. Moses' countenance shone brightly after his encounter with the Lord.

But what is the source of a happy countenance? Is it not the Lord, shining in our heart? David proclaimed, "They looked at him (the Lord) and were lightened (Hebrew—to sparkle, be cheerful)" (Ps. 34:5).

The Bible describes God as the Sun of Righteousness "arising with healing in his wings." If we would have a shining face, we must have the SON shining in our heart!

Final thought: A SON-filled heart makes for a happy face, and a happy face makes for a healthy home! Fill your heart with Him, and both your countenance and your words will be like sunshine in your home!

Day 80

PROVERBS 15:30

"The light of the eyes rejoiceth the heart: and a good report maketh the bones fat."

Wisdom in Our Face, Part 2

Our last devotional spoke of the affective and reflective nature of our face. We discovered that our face both affects our home and reflects what is in our heart.

Sometime we lose our smile and become frowning parents. Problems at work or with our spouse, difficult children, sickness, or a tired body all tend to wipe the joy from our face. Yet, these may be symptoms of a deeper problem in our heart.

A frowning face is often the result of sin within! Occasionally my wife asks, "Why are you frowning?" Usually it is because I'm either worried (the sin of faithlessness), frustrated (sin of a wrong focus), I have too much to do and not enough time to do it (the sin of overcommitment), or I simply frown out of habit (I've frowned so many months that even though I have nothing about which to frown, I still do)! Whichever may be the case, I am not reflecting a heart that is filled with the joy of the Lord, and it affects my family! What must I do? I must deal with my sin.

First, I must search my heart and the Word to find the reason for my joyless face. Then, I must confess and forsake my sin and ask God to "restore unto me the joy of my salvation" (Ps. 51:12). Finally, I must get my focus back on my All-sufficient God and glorious Savior and bless Him for His many benefits (Ps. 103).

Final thought: As the Jewish leaders took note that the disciples "had been with Jesus," so will your children rejoice when your face reflects the glory of the Lord!

Day 81

PROVERBS 15:31

"The ear that heareth the reproof of life abideth among the wise."

Wisdom in Helping Children Listen

Wise children listen, and wise parents can do much to help produce good listeners! It is incumbent on parents to insure that their children "hear the reproof of life." But how do we get youth, who have a thousand things to distract them, to listen?

First, children listen to those they respect. We gain their respect by our consistent godliness and by our spiritual wisdom. Children who listen have parents who earn that respect! Their children see them on their knees and note that their feet follow the path of their prayers! They are faithful in church, faithful in reading the Word, and faithful in conforming their lives to the Word. Their language is holy; their tempers are under control; and their discipline is consistent, loving, and biblical.

Such parents are also respected for their spiritual wisdom. Parents who seldom read the Word or who know little more of its teaching than the child will not be respected when they admonish their child. When they quote the Bible to their child, he thinks, "Who are you to quote the Bible? I never see you read it. You never have devotions. You seldom go to church." Lot's children lost respect for both his life and his wisdom, and in their deepest hour of crisis they mocked their father and would not respect him, to their own doom. Lot and his family paid dearly for his failure.

Second, children listen to those who care about them. Wise parents get involved in their children's lives. They play with them, laugh with them, cry with them, go places with them, hug them, love them, write notes to them, and listen to them! They build such a close relationship that the children listen carefully to the parent's words. Though the child may appear to reject those words, they go down into his heart and eventually spring up as obedience.

Final thought: Live consistently before your child and listen carefully when he talks, and you will be listened to when you admonish.

Day 82

PROVERBS 16:1

"The preparations of the heart in man, and the answer of the tongue, is from the Lord."

Wisdom in Heart Preparation

Thousands prepare their face each morning but forget about their heart! In Hebrew this verse reads, "The preparations of the heart belong to man, but the answer of the tongue is from the Lord." It is your responsibility to prepare your heart to face each day. It is God's part to use your prepared heart to the greatest advantage.

Here is both a promise and a principle. The promise is that if we adequately prepare our hearts, God will give us the very words we need for every eventuality we will face this day. The principle is that victory in our life depends on how well we prepare our hearts. If we don't prepare our hearts, God will not speak through us as we instruct our children. What a fearful thought. It is imperative that we prepare our hearts!

How do we make daily "preparations of the heart"? First, we read God's Word every morning. Second, we record what we learn about His character that day. Third, we memorize a verse for the day. Fourth, we meditate on that verse all day. Fifth, we review past "Heart Preparations" that we have recorded (to keep them fresh in our mind). Finally, we pray and ask God to use His Word in our lives this day.

Final thought: Only the prepared heart can impact a child's heart.

Day 83

PROVERBS 16:3

"Commit thy works unto the Lord, and thy thoughts shall be established."

Wisdom in Trusting

Worry is the sin of not trusting, and like all sin, it is far more than "wrong." It is a destructive force in life.

Worry wounds us mentally. The Greek word means "a divided mind." Charles Bridges comments, "An unsettled mind is a serious evil…. The memory is confused, the judgment undecided, the will unsteady." John Edmund Haggai adds, "Worry divides the mind between worthwhile interests and damaging thoughts…. Worry divides the understanding; therefore convictions are shallow and changeable. Worry divides the faculty of perception; therefore observations are faulty and even false."

Worry wounds us physically. It has been tied to heart trouble, high blood pressure, some forms of asthma, rheumatism, ulcers, cold, thyroid malfunction, migraines…and most stomach disorders (Dr. Edward Padolsky, in Stop Worrying and Get Well).

Worry also wounds the soul. Sinful worry immobilizes. A worrier is afraid to make a move for fear of what might happen. Worry affects our conversation, our discipline, and our planning. Thus, Solomon writes, "Commit thy works unto the Lord, and thy thoughts (plans) shall be established."

Parents who do not trust the Lord in every circumstance make poor decisions, are preoccupied with their own pondering, give wrong advice to their children, and model a "live-by-the-seat-of-your-pants" philosophy to their offspring. Their thoughts are not *established*, a Hebrew word meaning "to stand up" or "to be certain."

Final thought: When we confess our sin of not trusting and commit our works to Him, the burden is lifted, the mind is eased, the thoughts composed, and the parent is able to manage a functional home because he is at peace in his mind.

Day 84

PROVERBS 16:7

"When a man's ways please the Lord, he maketh even his enemies to be at peace with him."

Wisdom in Building Relationships

All relationships in life are based on one relationship! Peace with family, neighbors, friends, and enemies is based on our relationship with the Lord.

But doesn't this run contrary to reality? Many people who have a right relationship still find themselves the objects of hatred and persecution. This was especially clear in the life of Jesus Christ. Charles Bridges deals with this question by showing that the righteous do have enemies, but God sometimes restrains the wrath of those enemies and other times allows it because it will bring Him the most glory.

Bishop Patrick stated, "The best way for our enemies to be reconciled to us, is for us to be reconciled to God." When our ways please the Lord, parents and children, who otherwise might take offense, will have no grounds on which to act. Our very relationship with the Lord will protect us from making fleshly decisions, from making rash statements, or from using hurtful words.

Thus, it is vital that we spend quality time with the Lord and let His Word take root in our heart so that we may abound "therein with thanksgiving" (Col. 2:7).

Final thought: "Great peace have they which love thy law: and nothing shall offend them" (Ps. 119:165). Peace in your home is proof of peace in your heart.

Day 85

PROVERBS 16:12

"It is an abomination to kings to commit wickedness: for the throne is established by righteousness."

Wisdom in Righteous Respect

As the throne is established by righteousness, so a righteous parent will establish his leadership in the family.

Verse 12 is the third of four verses (vv. 10–13) that can be called "God's manual for kings." These verses show what God requires of kings, that they may be a blessing to their people. If the standard is neglected, the people suffer.

The same is true of a parent and his child. Solomon's wise handling of two women who claimed the same child is noteworthy. First Kings 3:26–28 tells us that the people "feared the king: for they saw that the wisdom of God was in him, to do judgment." As a result, Israel experienced her greatest glory under Solomon (Israel was "established" under Solomon).

Is this not a parent's greatest need? If we exude the wisdom of God and the righteousness of God, our children will "fear the king" and our home will experience the glory of God! But where do we get such wisdom and righteousness? It comes by being filled with the most righteously wise words ever spoken, the Word of God. When we are filled with and controlled by the Word, our homes will be established.

Final thought: Respect is earned, not forced. It is earned by the righteous words, life, and wisdom of the parent.

Day 86

PROVERBS 16:16

"How much better is it to get wisdom than gold! And to get understanding rather to be chosen than silver!

Wisdom in Our Priorities

Solomon's statement flies in the face of modern thought. Man's pursuit of gold has left him little time for true wisdom. Yet, most parents would agree that wisdom is more important than gold. Most would agree that heaven is more important than earth, that the soul is more valuable than the body, and that eternity is more important than time, but we fail to live what we say we believe. Our priorities are often at odds with what we confess.

Fathers put their job before their children. They are seldom home, or when they are home, they are preoccupied with other things. They excuse their lack of time with the children by saying they are "providing" for them. Yet, the children need their parents, not their gold.

Fathers and mothers are often guilty of emphasizing the body over the soul. They encourage their children to spend hours in sports and seldom mention devotions, Bible study, or Scripture memory. They spend their money buying uniforms, paying athletic fees, and burning gas to practice and games, but they think it's terrible to spend a few dollars for a youth activity or to take their child to Wednesday night youth meetings.

We too often allow our children to become so busy with earthly activities, homework, sports, being with their friends, shopping, and chores that they have little time to invest in eternal things.

How often do you ask your children about their devotions? How often do they see you having your devotions? How often do you challenge them to exercise their mind to memorize Scripture?

Final thought: What priorities do we practice? Are we so busy in the pursuit of gold that we have failed to find wisdom and understanding?

Day 87

PROVERBS 16:20

"He that handleth a matter wisely shall find good: and whoso trusteth in the Lord, happy is he."

Wisdom in Problem Solving

Every parent is a problem solver, but every problem is not wisely solved. David illustrates both wisdom and foolishness in solving his problems. When faced with an invasion of the Philistines in the Valley of Rephaim, David inquired of the Lord and was rewarded with victory (2 Sam. 5:19, 23). Years later as king, rather than seeking the Lord, he numbered the people to see if he had the strength to win a battle. This seemed logical enough. Does not a king count his troops to be sure he outnumbers the enemy? Yet God rebuked him for his logical act because it was motivated by fear and a lack of trust in the Lord.

When we solve problems with our children, we can handle them wisely or foolishly. The wise way is simple: turn to the Word and pray for wisdom. The foolish way is likewise simple: use human reasoning and give culturally accepted advice.

If we really believe the Word is sufficient for every problem, then we will use it as the basis of our counsel. The Word is not meant to be learned only but to be lived! When counseling, "What does the Bible say?" should be our first thought.

Two truths guide the wise counselor: 1) The Sufficiency of God's Word (our children need no other counsel than its laws—Ps. 119:24); and 2) The Supremacy of God's Word (we must submit to its teaching and conform our lives to its injunctions).

Final thought: The wise parent always asks, "How does the Bible say we should handle this situation?"

P R O V E R B S   1 6 : 2 4

"Pleasant words are as an honeycomb, sweet to the soul, and health to the bones."

Wisdom in Speech

Honey is good and good for you—a rare combination! Generally, if it tastes good, it is not healthy. If it tastes like cardboard, then it is good for you. Thus, honey is used in the Bible as the supreme symbol of the Word of God. David exclaimed, "How sweet are thy words unto my taste! Yea, sweeter than honey to my mouth" (Ps. 119:103). In another Psalm he stated that God's Word is sweeter than honey and the honeycomb (Ps. 19:10). Like honey, God's Word is both good, and good for you!

So are pleasant words. They are both "sweet to the soul, and health to the bones." Do we realize the power of our words? We can both kill and give life with the tongue. A wrong word can destroy a child for life, while pleasant words can give him spiritual health. We must be sure our words are saturated with His honey.

But what are pleasant words? When they are words of counsel, sympathy, or encouragement, they are medicinal and sweet. "But much more are the pleasant words of God both sweet and wholesome" (Charles Bridges). If you would be satisfied and spiritually healthy, then drink deep of God's honey.

Final thought: Pleasure and healing flow from the man who is full of God's Word. Let your words be "honey" for your children.

Day 89

"Pleasant words are as an honeycomb, sweet to the soul, and health to the bones."

Wisdom in Giving Hope

Not all children need to be "preached to" when they do wrong! First Thessalonians 5:14 identifies three types of problem children: the unruly (disorderly/rebellious), the feebleminded (small souled; easily discouraged); and the weak. Significantly, each type is dealt with differently. The rebellious must be warned (admonished); the feebleminded must be comforted (to come near to and encourage); the weak must be strengthened (to prop up, stand up beside). In each case the idea of hope is very strong. Even the word *warn* is a Greek word that generally means to counsel with biblical instruction. The last two verbs (comfort and support) both imply the act of encouragement. Youth who are easily discouraged especially need hope. Berating them for their failure may well doom them to further failure. Sin and failure kills the spirit of many.

It is our job to be "health to the bones" even when our child has committed the vilest of sins! When Jesus met the woman taken in adultery, he did not berate her (though her sin was grievous); rather He told her that He did not accuse her and to "go and sin no more." There was hope and health in that statement.

Final thought: Use pleasant words when dealing with defeated youth. You may well be the means of saving them from destruction.

Day 90

PROVERBS 16:25

"There is a way that seemeth right unto a man, but the end thereof are the ways of death."

Wisdom in Dealing with Naiveté & Delusion

Youth, like all of us, have sinful natures. But unlike adults, childhood naiveté magnifies their problem. Their sin nature gives them a desire for wrong, and their lack of knowledge and understanding greases the way.

It is our job to show our children that what may seem right might actually lead to death! We must realize that "All the ways of a man are clean in his own eyes" (Prov. 16:2). Even the persecutors of believers think they are doing God service (John 16:2). Lying seems better than truth when it will help us escape trouble. Cheating seems better than making a bad grade and disappointing our parents. All our sin seems to be so good and beneficial, "but the end thereof are the ways of death."

Parents must continually remind youth of the scriptural consequences of evil. Use biblical illustrations: David's sin with Bathsheba seemed right to David, but it cost him his son! Keeping the best of the sheep to sacrifice to God seemed to be right to Saul, but it cost him his throne. Scripture is full of such illustrations. Further, use current events to remind youth that what seemed right destroyed a life. (A night of drinking leads to death, etc. Your newspapers are full of such information.)

Final thought: Immaturity seldom looks beyond the present. Instill in your children the fear of the Lord and the fear of sin!

Day 91

PROVERBS 16:27
"An ungodly man diggeth up evil: and in his lips there is as a burning fire."

Wisdom in Dealing with Unforgetful Youth

Homes can be destroyed by fire. But the fire mentioned here is caused by the tongue of one who refuses to forget a past offense by another family member. Children are notorious at forgetting their chores or homework, but many never forget the past failures of a brother, sister, or parent. Sadly, some parents are also guilty of reminding a spouse or child of long dead sins. How do we deal with such discord in our home?

First, we should use the language of the Bible in describing this sin. God calls those who dig up evil, "ungodly," or (simply put) not like God. When God forgives, He forgets. He promises, "Your sins and iniquities will I remember no more" (Heb. 8:12). Thus, digging up past (or even present) sin is un-Godlike. The word translated *ungodly* is, if possible, even stronger than the word fool. Those who dig up past sin are like grave robbers and arsonists! They bring up dead issues and use them to start a burning fire. Their lips delight in reminding others of their past failures.

Second, we must note the origin of digging up the past. The burning fire in our lips is set on fire of hell! Satan is the slayer of men, and he often uses our tongues as his weapon! Thus, James says that the tongue that sows discord is born in hell (James 3:6). This is not a pleasant description.

Are our homes fireproof? Do we forgive and forget? Do we allow our children to remind everyone of their sibling's past failures? Do we continually remind our children of their past failure, or do we let dead sins lie?

Final thought: Face the sin of remembering past sin with the Word. Use Scripture to bring conviction and douse the fire of hell. Make your home fireproof.

Day 92

PROVERBS 16:28

"A froward man soweth strife: and a whisperer separateth chief friends."

Wisdom in Dealing with a Divisive Tongue

Today's devotional continues the thought from yesterday dealing further with destructive speech. This verse focuses on its consequences. Destructive speech can destroy the closest relationship, especially when the offender intends to spread strife. Sadly, children often learn to be divisive from their parents! Unthinking parents may be guilty of criticizing the teacher, the preacher, or others in front of their children. Their children take up the offense and soon lose respect for the target of gossip. Little do they realize that their parents have taught them the art of destructive slander!

Again, note God's language in describing the slanderer. Divisive speech is characteristic of the froward. This word can be translated "perverse, malicious, or crooked." It is connected with lying or fraudulent speech. The idea behind the word is to change or twist a fact so that it appears to mean something else entirely. Its intention is to sow strife. God calls a slanderer froward or crooked!

The word *whisperer* means "to roll to pieces." Thus, the whisperer will not let a thing die! He will continue to bring it up until he has at last turned friend against friend. A whisperer is a gossip. He repeats the bad that he hears to others.

We must be careful that we identify such behavior in our home and show youth what God thinks of this practice. Further, we must be certain that we do not practice it or allow it in our home or in our church.

Final thought: Those who bend truth are themselves bent (crooked), and bent parents will produce bent children!

Day 93

PROVERBS 16:32

"He that is slow to anger is better than the mighty; and he that ruleth his spirit than he that taketh a city."

Wisdom in Self-Control

A man who captures a city can lose it to a stronger foe. Self-control, however, can never be conquered. Looking at this verse in reverse we realize that losing one's temper defeats a man. We always lose when we lose control. Here is a fateful warning: A lost temper may lose a home!

Those who cannot control their spirit cannot control their family. Some seek to control their children by shouting, demanding, and threatening. The wise control them by controlling themselves. Far more "mighty" is the latter. Charles Bridges put it this way: "Instead of having rule over their spirit, they are captives, not conquerors." The same goes for a raging child. He must be taught that he demonstrates his weakness, not his strength, when he loses his temper.

The word translated *slow to anger* is actually the Hebrew for "long-nosed!" It is in contrast to the heavy breathing and snorting of an angry man. The "short-nosed" feel they have good reason to be angry (Jonah, for example). Parents may feel the same justification toward a disobedient child—it's a disgrace to put up with wrong! Thus, they excuse their temper as "righteous indignation." The raging child may think his fits of temper will get him what he wants. He must be shown otherwise.

James commands us to bridle our tongue and so check our passions. Paul reminds us to "let all bitterness, and wrath, and anger…be put away from you, with all malice" (Eph. 4:31). Self-controlled fathers are more likely to have controlled homes than an out-of-control father.

Final thought: A raging parent is a weak parent in danger of losing his home.

Day 94

PROVERBS 17:5

"Whoso mocketh the poor reproacheth his Maker: and he that is glad at calamities shall not be unpunished."

Wisdom in Showing Respect

Youth are notorious for not respecting the feelings of others. In their naiveté they laugh and scoff when someone fails or makes a dumb remark. They laugh at the out-of-style clothes of the poor, or they scoff at the awkwardness of the un-athletic child.

Even more they enjoy the problems and punishments of their enemies. Though most of us would never admit it, our selfish spirit may inwardly laugh at the news that our enemy has fallen. Yet, even this is sin!

Parents must teach their children to respect others—even their enemies— regardless of their talent, appearance, dress, race, or position in life. How do we do this?

First, use Scripture. Make Scripture the final authority for all counsel in the home. Use this verse to teach respect. Other verses that teach the same truth include Proverbs 24:17–18; Psalm 35:11–14, and Romans 12:20–21.

Second, remind your child that we are all created in the image of God. Thus, when they mock others, they are really mocking God. To mock God's image is a sin of the deepest type (Gen. 9:6)! To mock God's image by mocking others is to mock their creator God!

Final thought: Teach your children to pray for each other by name, rather than mock each other in shame.

Day 95

PROVERBS 17.17
"A friend loveth at all times, and a brother is born for adversity."

Wisdom in Friendship with Our Children

Parents must be more than authority figures. They must be friends to their children. Friendship is the product of spending quality and quantity time with children. Christ came down from heaven to live among men, to call out a people for His name, and to call them friends (John 15:14–15). He created friendships by spending both quality and quantity time with His disciples. He was more than an authority figure to them. He was their friend, their confidant, and their teacher, and He always had time for his friends! John later wrote that he had seen, heard, and handled the Lord. His experience was one of an intimate friendship.

Genuine followers of the Lamb will spend time with their children. They will get involved in their personal lives. They will play with them, pray with them, and counsel them. They will praise them for their good and admonish them for their weakness and sin.

But how should we treat them when they disobey? First, we should confront them with their sin. Thus, "a brother is born for adversity." Friendship confronts failure in a kind way and offers biblical steps to overcome it. Refusing to confront our children is a sign of contempt, not a sign of love! Second, we listen when they talk. We do not quickly rebuke them for their words or actions. Instead, we lovingly listen to their heart and weigh our counsel. Finally, we show them we love and respect them even in their sin ("a friend loveth at all times"). This demonstrates that we are not ashamed of them though we may be disappointed with their ways.

Final thought: Come down from your authority perch and enjoy your children so you can be a trusted friend in their times of adversity.

Day 96

PROVERBS 17:22

"A merry heart doeth good like a medicine: but a broken spirit drieth the bones."

Wisdom in Outlook

A merry heart is here contrasted with a broken spirit. While God wants us to have a broken and contrite heart (Ps. 51:17) in regard to our sin, He does not want us to have a despondent and negative spirit. The contrast in this verse is in regards to one's attitude and outlook in life. We are to be happy, excited, positive, and encouraging. It is not fitting that a child of a victorious God should live in despair and gloom. We have every reason to rejoice. Yet, some believers live in the dark and dank cave of despair and gloom. They know how to complain, but they have forgotten how to praise.

Beware the broken spirit! It looks at the dark side of life and broods over circumstances. It is quick to complain but slow to smile and laugh. The Bible warns that it will dry up the bones. Physically, a negative spirit will drain our energy, sap our strength, and rob us of vitality and life!

Further, a negative outlook will dry up our spiritual vitality, because we fail to see the power and majesty of God. We lose the joy of seeing answered prayer. Instead of praising, our tongue complains. And what are the results? Not only are we the worse, but so is our family. God dies in their soul! Christianity shrivels to an ancient creed to be slavishly memorized and served. Christ is perceived as the source of misery rather than the God of all joy. The children of such a home prefer to visit their friends' homes and see their own home as a castle of doom!

Final thought: You can be a saving medicine or a somber mortician to your family. Look up! Gather in His sunshine, and spread His healing power to your home.

PROVERBS 18.1

"Through desire a man, having separated himself, seeketh and intermeddleth with all wisdom."

Wisdom in Admitting We Are Wrong

This is a verse that is not very well understood. On the surface it seems to say that a man that wants wisdom should seek it in solitude. However, that is not really what the verse means. Far from encouraging solitude, this verse actually condemns the schismatic attitude of the man that goes his own way. One commentary explains the verse as saying "a divisive man seeks an opportunity for a quarrel; he rails against all sound policy" (The New American Commentary).

I remember hearing a pastor tell the story of a man in his church who was very contrary. He finally told the man, "I believe that if the deacons passed a resolution that the sky was blue, you'd disagree with that too!" Some people are never happy unless they are contrary. Some parents irritate all around them (including their children) by bugging them over inconsequential things. They are stubborn and refuse to admit when they are wrong.

A divisive parent always insists he is right even when wrong. At the bottom of this attitude lies a prideful heart. This person will disagree with simple reasoning just because they want to be different. Are you that parent? Do you have a conflict with your children or spouse right now simply because you enjoy being right or contrary? Is it because you are proud? You may claim that your disagreement is over principle, but it has been said that "many an angry man has masqueraded as a righteous crusader." Many a divisive parent has masqueraded this way as well.

Final thought: Sometimes we show our wisdom by admitting we are wrong!

Day 98

PROVERBS 18:10
"The name of the Lord is a strong tower: the righteous runneth into it, and is safe."

Wisdom in Trusting God's Name

So often in times of trial we trust our own machinations. Solomon mentions this type of thinking in the next verse. He pictures the rich man, who wrongly believes his wealth is his strong city with impenetrable walls. Like that rich man, we seek to find our own ways out of life's troubles.

The righteous have found a better way—the strong tower of God's name! When the righteous face impossible trials, rather than trust to their own worry, fret, preoccupations, and devices, they have learned to call on the name of the Lord. They run into it and are safe. That is, they trust Him rather than their own wits. They rest. They pray. They reflect on His character.

Our home must be a secure castle for our children, but that castle must be protected by the strong tower of God's name! Psalm 9:10 says, "And they that know thy name will put their trust in thee: for thou, Lord, hast not forsaken them that seek thee." Do we know God's names? Do our children know how to use His names in times of trouble, doubt, and fear?

The Psalmist in Psalm 91 speaks of the power and value of using God's various names in different situations. In the appendix we have printed portions of this Psalm and have listed many names of God and their meanings. Teach these names to your children and show them how to call upon the appropriate ones for victory in their life. For example, when faced with a family need, have the family call upon God as El-Shaddai (All Sufficient God), or El Elyon (Most High God), or Yahweh (Lord/Jehovah).

Final thought: When building your home, don't forget the strong tower!

Day 99

PROVERBS 18.13
"He that answereth a matter before he heareth it, it is folly and shame unto him."

Wisdom in Reserving Judgment

The fool jumps to conclusions. Then, when he is proven wrong, he is shamed. We know this, yet how often do we put on our jumping shoes?! Sadly, we react rather than act. Job's friend, Elihu, considerately restrained himself until he had thoroughly heard the matter (Job 32:4, 10–11). Better by far that we gather information before we come to conclusions.

To reserve judgment is to show wisdom, but it also displays humility. Those who quickly judge a matter pride themselves in their astute judgment. They don't need facts; their intuition is so ironclad that they know the answer before they hear the question! Potiphar imprisoned Joseph because he failed to get the facts. He let his jealousy and wrath interfere with sound judgment. Yet, our omniscient God examined Adam before He pronounced judgment. He came down to see Babel and Sodom prior to their destruction. Does our knowledge exceed the All-Wise and Knowing Savior?

We quickly judge our children without listening to their explanation. When we do listen, we don't always really listen because our mind is already made up. We assume the worst without considering that other circumstances may be at work. We would do better to humbly confess we are not all-wise and gather the facts before we react. Better that we truly listen and weigh the matter before we judge. Many a parent has made a rash statement or imposed a rash punishment before he knew all the facts. Then, rather than admit the wrong, he compounds the problem by stubbornly sticking to his judgment—to his own shame and the hurt of his child.

Final thought: He who is wise does not trust his eyes!

Day 100

PROVERBS 18:17

"He that is first in his own cause seemeth just; but his neighbour cometh and searcheth him."

Wisdom in Listening

This passage parallel's yesterday's—he who is wise does not trust his eyes, but neither does he trust his ears! Have you noticed that there are always two sides to a story? The first sounds so right, so true that surely this person is in the right and the other wrong! Yet, if we would delay our judgment until we heard the other side, we would realize that everything is not black and white! How often has a tale of an uncaring boss or a broken home roused our sympathy? But a close look at the other side of the story revealed the error of a hasty, one-sided judgment. Wisdom has taught us to see both sides.

Is it not also true that we cannot see our own problems with perfect accuracy? Where our own name or credit is concerned, our argument "seemeth just." We rush in first with our own tale. We rationalize and reason ourselves righteous! But, according to this proverb, the first tale is good, until the second is heard. Our friend comes, examines us, exposes our failure, and puts us to shame. Saul convinced himself that he was right in sparing the best of the sheep—until his "neighbor" came and exposed his sin. In our own case we should guard against a self-justifying spirit.

Husbands and wives need to listen to the other side. Parents need to truly listen to their children. Our spouse and our children often see us better than we see ourselves!

Final thought: Listen carefully to both sides of a case—especially when you are one of the sides!

Day 101

PROVERBS 18.24

"A man that hath friends must shew himself friendly: and there is a friend that sticketh closer than a brother."

Wisdom in Depending on Friends

This verse has proven difficult for translators. The word translated *must show himself friendly* is actually a single word that has two meanings: "to break in pieces/to shatter" or "to shout in triumph." Most scholars thus interpret the first half of the verse to say, "A man of many friends shouts in triumph" (that is, he proudly boasts of how popular he is), or "A man of many friends will come to ruin" (that is, he will have more heartaches because "friends" often turn against us). If either of these translations is accurate, then the first half of the verse is in contrast to the latter half, which states that there is a friend who will never let us down. In other words, a true friend is a rare and treasured jewel.

Regardless of the translation problems, the verse teaches that it is better to have one true friend than a multitude of sycophants, who will turn on us when they disagree with our actions! Often it is true that those who seem to butter you up the most will become your enemy just as quickly. Thus, we must be careful of our friends. Choose them wisely.

A wise parent will trust in his One True Friend (the Lord Jesus Christ) more than in a hundred human friends. Why? Mankind is subject to selfishness and is thus prone to forsake us in our time of deepest need. Our best friend may disappoint us in time of trouble. Our children may be overly polite only to gain a selfish end. Some deeply hurt their parents and say cruel things to them. But Christ will never disappoint! Make Him your best friend.

Final thought: Be a true friend to your children—even when they fail!

Day 102

PROVERBS 19:3

"The foolishness of man perverteth his way: and his heart fretteth against the Lord."

Wisdom in Confronting Sin

It is man's nature to sin and to blame God for it! Yet, it is his own foolishness that perverts his way. Here we see a man blaming ("fretting against") God for his own perversion. He might say, "It's not my fault that I have these strong desires. I can't help it. God made me this way." Such is the thinking of modern society. Charles Manson once remarked that he did no wrong in the Sharon Tate murders because "he felt like it." Surely, if he felt like it, God must have given him those desires (so he tragically reasoned)!

While we see the folly of such a statement, do not our children (and their parents) often say essentially the same thing? "I couldn't help it. So and so made me do it." We may defend our own children by saying, "It's the crowd she was with." Such statements dodge the issue of man's own foolishness perverting his way. The wise parent will help her children take responsibility for their own sin and show them what God says about it in the Bible. We call it "stretching a point," but the Bible calls it lying. It isn't "cheating;" it's stealing. We need to use biblical terminology for sin. We need children who willingly confess, "I have sinned," "I have disobeyed God's Word," "I have lied," etc. We need parents who will not make excuses for their children's failures and sin.

Further, we must show them that they can choose not to sin! First Corinthians 10:13 plainly states, "…but God is faithful, who will not suffer you to be tempted above that ye are able; but will with the temptation also make a way to escape…."

Final thought: Help youth face their sinfulness squarely, accept the blame, name it for what it really is, and confess it.

Day 103

PROVERBS 19:5

"A false witness shall not be unpunished, and he that speaketh lies shall not escape."

Wisdom in Dealing with Lies

How big can a lie become? "It's only a little fib," someone says. "It's just a white lie." "I was only joking." These are but a few of the cover-ups for what God calls lying. If "a truthful witness delivereth souls" (Prov. 14:25), a false witness destroys them. Satan's lie brought about the fall of all mankind, and the Bible has many more illustrations of the destructive force of a lie.

Charles Bridges stated: "Strict attention to truth forms a primary point in Christian education. The boundary line must never be trifled with. Not even a child can pass it without paying a price. It will soon lose its respect, if it isn't reverenced at any cost and under all circumstances. A child must never be allowed to play with a lie. It must constantly be pressed upon him that anything less than truth is a lie. Even if no one is deceived by it, a habit is fostered, and we can't tell how big it will actually become."

Small white lies grow into larger ones. Soon, respect for truth is lost. Lying will eventually banish the fear of being under oath. It will be excused to cover up sin. It will ultimately be used to destroy a life! This happens by degrees, and it often begins in the home.

Final thought: Do not allow lying in your home. Call your children on it and chasten them while there is hope!

Day 104

PROVERBS 19:11

"The discretion of a man deferreth his anger; and it is his glory to pass over a transgression."

Wisdom in Personal Attacks

When others sin, it is right to confront them in a spirit of meekness. However, when one sins against us, it is often best to let it pass! The discrete man (literally a man of insight, intelligence) will delay his anger. He will "pass over" (cover) sins against him.

But it is not so of the proud. The pride of man will glow white-hot when someone dares to offend him. He will not hold his anger but will be quick to lash out and reveal his ego!

Someone has called anger "temporary madness." We yield to angry outbursts or act impulsively because we are not guarded by humility. Men are especially prone to this temptation. They are likely to feel that overlooking an offense shows a lack of courage and manhood. But Solomon declares it to be a strength rather than a weakness to be able to graciously bear things that offend us. Angry outbursts also fail to show the Spirit of Christ. Isaiah 53:7 tells us that "as a sheep before her shearers is dumb, so he openeth not his mouth." Yet, was there ever one that was manlier than our Lord?

It isn't good character and strength that causes us to lash out at others; it is poor character and weakness that does so. In so doing, we lose the respect of those we are seeking to raise for the Lord.

Final thought: A closed mouth and a meek spirit can glorify God more than a thousand words!

Day 105

PROVERBS 19:12

"The king's wrath is as the roaring of a lion; but his favour is as dew upon the grass."

Wisdom in Leadership

Everything a king does is magnified in the eyes of men. His anger is much hotter, his failures much more grievous, and his kindness far more glorious than any other in the kingdom. Why? He is the leader. He is in the spotlight. His subjects' lives are tied to his actions, motives, and character. In this way the king of the realm is like the king of the forest. The prophet Amos asks, "The lion hath roared, who will not fear?" (Amos 3:8). The animals of the forest run in every direction at the sound. So it is with all leaders. So it will be in the home.

A father (or mother) can be a lion or he can be as dew upon the grass! He can lead his family in one of two ways: by fear or by favor! Better it is that he learn the power of dew than the power of the lion. The lion frightens and causes death and dread. The tiny dew refreshes and brings life and vigor.

What is the dew that refreshes a home? In this instance it is called the *favor of the king*. The Hebrew means "that which is pleasing or acceptable." Thus the word *dew* refers to that which encourages and nourishes your family. It is kindness and words of affirmation. Are you the refreshing dew or the roaring lion to your children? One tears down, while the other builds up! Are you a father or mother that roars in anger or screams in displeasure? Do you storm and stomp, throw things, or grab your spouse or child? Do you "nuke" or nourish your family? Do you lead by rage or by righteousness?

Final thought: The lion rules the forest, roaring to and fro; while the dew, though unnoticed, makes the forest grow!

Day 106

PROVERBS 19:15

"Slothfulness casteth into a deep sleep; and an idle soul shall suffer hunger."

Wisdom in Fervency

If a lazy parent is bad, the vice is even worse in a Christian parent! We have every reason to be fervent in spirit because we serve the Lord God—the King of Kings and Lord of Lords! Paul reminds believers that we must not be "slothful in business" but rather be "fervent in spirit; serving the Lord" (Rom. 12:11).

A lazy parent is slovenly in discipline. He lets problems go without counsel because he is too lazy to confront the problem, to look up Scripture that may help, to use his mental energy to think through the situation, and to take the time to counsel his family. He would rather read the paper, watch the football game, or let his wife solve the problem.

A lazy parent is slovenly in correction and in counsel. He would rather punish or reprimand than to counsel or encourage. It takes energy and time to counsel children and help them overcome their problem. So, he carelessly lashes with his tongue or avoids the problem altogether.

A lazy parent is slovenly in spending time with children. He doesn't have time to help them with homework. He is too tired to go to their plays, their ballgames, or school functions. He is too tired to play with them after school, to pray with them, to have devotions with them, or to help them with their devotions.

A lazy parent is slovenly in his own spiritual disciplines. His children seldom see him pray, read God's Word, or go to church.

Final thought: Check your energy level. Are you excited about God? Are you fervently serving the Lord? Are you slothful in parenting?

Day 107

PROVERBS 19:20

"Hear counsel, and receive instruction, that thou mayest be wise in thy latter end."

Wisdom in Listening, Part 1

This verse cuts several ways. First, it applies to you as the counselee. Second it applies to your children. Third, it applies to you as the counselor.

As the counselee, we must be ready to listen and learn. We do make mistakes! Parents do mishandle situations. Parents do not know all the answers. But pride is the chief enemy of learning and accepting instruction. "Who are they to teach me? What do they know more than me?" These are the words of pride, and they block the door to future wisdom!

Second, our children must learn to listen. And constantly they need to be reminded! Have them memorize and quote this verse when they do not pay attention. Admonish inattentiveness with Scripture! Solomon tells us in Ecclesiastes 11:10 that "childhood and youth are vanity." That is, most youth waste their time. Present gratification is their main object with little regard for the future. In sarcasm Solomon tells the youth to "walk in the ways of thine heart, and in the sight of thine eyes" (Eccles. 11:9). In other words, "Don't listen; go happily on your way!" Then he adds: "But know thou, that for all these things God will bring thee into judgment."

Final thought: Use Scripture to teach attentiveness. If your children will not listen to God, they will not listen to you!

Day 108

PROVERBS 19:20

"Hear counsel, and receive instruction, that thou mayest be wise in thy latter end."

Wisdom in Listening, Part 2

Yesterday we discussed two ways this verse may be applied: to you as the counselee and to your children. There is a third way you must apply this verse: to you as a counselor.

It is as important that parents listen to their children as it is for children to listen to their parents! Listening cuts both ways. The counselor who will not listen is set on pride! He assumes he has all the answers. However, if we do not listen carefully, we may miss the most vital direction for our counsel. Essentially, a parent is in the business of counseling, and one half (perhaps two thirds) of counseling is listening! Proverbs 18:13 reminds us, "He that answereth a matter before he heareth it, it is folly and shame unto him." Often our children tell us things that we do not even hear. We have already made up our minds. We have already judged them to be rebellious, disobedient, lazy, or incompetent. Yet, we have not carefully listened to what is in their hearts. Thus James admonishes us: "Let every man be swift to hear, slow to speak, slow to wrath" (James 1:19).

Good counselors are good listeners. They ask questions and listen carefully to the answers. They want to know what is in the heart.

Final thought: Turn your ears on before you engage your mouth.

Day 109

PROVERBS 19:21

"There are many devices in a man's heart; nevertheless the counsel of the Lord, that shall stand."

Wisdom in Counsel

Do you believe in the sufficiency of the Word? Do you practice it? This verse contrasts the devices of a man and the counsel of the Lord. Too often we depend on our own devices rather than the Word. We entice (or force) youth to obey rather than showing them the clear teachings of God's Word and challenging them to do what it says!

A "device" is a manipulative means of affecting behavior apart from the Word. For example, the parents of a rebellious teen at first used human devices to keep their child away from her ungodly friends. However, they soon realized the problem hadn't been solved. She couldn't see her friends, but her heart hadn't changed. They used external means to deal with an internal problem. Upon seeking biblical counsel, the teenager was saved and began a process of spiritual growth. Her parents realized that it was better to use the Word to affect her heart than to manipulate her to do what was right.

Devices may change behavior, but only God's Word can change the heart! Children must be shown which verses of Scripture they are disobeying and how their sin is really against God. Your words will last a day. God's Word will last for eternity.

Final thought: Only that correction anchored in God's Word will last.

Day 110

PROVERBS 19:22
"The desire of a man is his kindness: and a poor man is better than a liar."

Wisdom in Kind Truthfulness

Kindness and truth make the perfect couple! To be a kind liar is to be a deadly deceiver. To be an unkind judge is to be an ogre. Jesus stood for truth but still forgave the repentant. He denounced arrogance, pretence, and pride, but forgave the woman taken in adultery, fed the hungry, gave sight to the blind, wept over Jerusalem, and gave his life a ransom for many.

While it is important to "speak the truth," we must ever do so "in love" (Eph. 4:15). Balancing truth with love may be the most difficult of all Christian exercises. Yet, God's Word requires us to do just that. This balance is especially important for parents. You must never lie by glossing over a sin—whether it is in your life or that of your children. You are better off poor than to fail to confront sin. Second Timothy 3:16 reveals that the Bible is profitable for four things—one of them being reproof. This word means to bring a person under conviction. Thus, the Word is to be wisely and kindly used in our homes to show youth that they are guilty. Only this "kind confrontation" with the Word will bring conviction for sin and cause your children to appreciate you the more for loving them enough to use Scripture to illuminate their sin.

Final thought: The most attractive parents are those who kindly and consistently use Scripture to confront sin in their children's lives!

Day 111

PROVERBS 19:24

"A slothful man hideth his hand in his bosom, and will not so much as bring it to his mouth again."

Wisdom in the Daily Disciplines

Laziness affects more than one's job. It also affects one's spiritual growth. So debilitating is laziness that the slothful will not even provide for his noon meal! He would rather be hungry than use his energy to prepare a meal.

While we may think such laziness is inexcusable, does this not illustrate our spiritual laziness? Spiritual growth requires daily discipline and industry. Prayer is work. Having daily devotions is a struggle. It comes easy to no one, but the spiritually lazy will especially suffer. Lethargy will stop our hand from reaching out to partake of the "daily bread."

We can wish to live a fruitful life of prayer and devotions, yet fail to do so because of spiritual slothfulness. How sad at the end to "remember that all this was wished, yes, even resolved; yet not a bit of it accomplished" (Bridges).

Do you wish to have a better prayer life, a deeper devotional life, a greater intimacy with God? What keeps you from it? Is it the most deadly of sins—spiritual lethargy?

Do you wish that your children had a heart for God? Do you wish that they were more interested in spiritual things and less interested in the world? What hinders them? Is it the deadliest of sins—parents who wish but lack the diligence to keep up with their children's spiritual disciplines?

When prayer is cold and heartless, pray the more! When God's Word is dry and meaningless, meditate the more! Form habits of early energy. Turn wishing into action. Cultivate bodily activity.

Final thought: Spiritual laziness is a poison that only discipline can assuage!

Day 112

PROVERBS 19:27

"Cease, my son, to hear the instruction that causeth to err from the words of knowledge."

Wisdom in Education

In this verse, Christian parents see their responsibility in educating their children. We must teach them to cease listening to those philosophies that hinder obedience to the Word of God. The same words came from Christ: "Beware of false prophets" (Matt. 7:15), and "Take heed what ye hear" (Mark 4:24). All instruction is not truth, and that which is not truth is not true education! Worse, that which is not truth will lead youth astray and cause them to "err from the words of knowledge."

If secular education causes youth to err from the words of knowledge, then Christian education exists to enable youth to follow the words of knowledge! And the home is the heart of Christian education.

Thus, only that education which confronts youth with the very words of Scripture is truly Christian! It is not enough to tell children that they should not lie or that they should not steal or criticize; society tells them that. Instead, we must show them from the Words of Knowledge that they must replace lying with truth, replace stealing with labor, and replace gossip with wholesome words. When youth err from the words of knowledge, we must use the words of knowledge to reprove them of their sin. This is the heart of Christian education. Whether your child is homeschooled, goes to a Christian school, or attends a public school, it is the parents' responsibility to insure that their education is godly.

Final thought: Christian educators (whether at school or in the home) are not "Christianly educating" if they are not using the very words of knowledge to convict, correct, and instruct in righteous living (2 Tim. 3:16).

Day 113

PROVERBS 20:5

"Counsel in the heart of man is like deep water; but a man of understanding will draw it out."

Wisdom in Transparency

What is at the bottom of a child's heart is difficult to discover, but a wise parent will take the time to draw it out. Sadly, we are often too busy to know our children's hearts. They may have deep scars from troubles with friends. They may have deep-rooted sin problems that lead to habitual sin patterns. But instead of taking the time to draw out the deeper problem, we only attack the surface problem. In essence we place band-aids on boils!

Drawing out what a child really thinks requires four things: time, understanding, a listening ear, and personal transparency. Parents must spend quality time at meals, at play, driving their children to activities, and other informal moments to get to know the heart of their child. They must ask questions, probe, and allow the child to be transparent without judging or reacting to the words that come from the depths.

But, if we are to draw out the depths of a child's heart, we must also be willing to reveal the depths of our own hearts to our children. Only those parents who are transparent themselves will have transparent children! How gifted are you at sharing your frailties, failures, burdens, wishes, heartaches, and joys with your children? Do you ask them to pray for you? Do your show your frailties?

Final thought: Share the depths of your heart if you would plumb the depths of your child's heart.

Day 114

PROVERBS 20:8

"A king that sitteth in the throne of judgment scattereth away all evil with his eyes."

Wisdom in a Look

An admired leader needs but to look on the guilty to dispel their evil! Not so a weaker man. God often leads with the simple look of His eye! "The foolish shall not stand in thy sight" (Ps. 5:5). "His eyes behold, his eyelids try the children of men" (Ps. 11:4). "He ruleth by his power forever, his eyes behold the nations" (Ps. 66:7).

Further, the Lord reminds David, "I will guide thee with mine eye" (Ps. 32:8). Such is the power of a righteous leader! The power, however, is not in the eye, but in the admiration and love of others for the person behind the eye.

A godly, beloved parent or teacher can likewise stop many a misdeed with a simple look! When children admire their parents, a look may serve as correction better than words. Loud words and harsh threatening are the tools of the weak. Jesus was so gentle that "a bruised reed shall he not break, and smoking flax shall he not quench" (Matt. 12:20). Such is the power of a righteous life! Do youth so admire your character that you can lead with a look?

Final thought: The ability to govern with the eyes as easily as with the mouth is the true test of godly parenting!

Day 115

PROVERBS 20:11

"Even a child is known by his doings, whether his work be pure, and whether it be right."

Wisdom in Observation

A wise parent is an observing parent. He takes note of his child's habits, tempers, and deeds. Often the boy will tell in miniature what the man will one day be. No parent will pass over little faults. If a child is deceitful, quarrelsome, stubborn, or selfish, it must be wisely dealt with from the Word. Children must be led to see the ugly future of their early sin.

First, a parent should write each child's name separately on paper and beside each list areas where that child needs to grow.

Second, the parents should pray for the child in each of these specific areas. Our prayer should be two-fold: that God would do a work in his heart and life to change the child and that we would have wisdom in dealing with the child from Scripture in each of these areas.

Third, use specific Scripture with each child to help them see their sins and provide them with steps to overcome them.

Fourth, exercise patience, realizing that oak trees don't grow overnight! Augustine's mother had a difficult time while he was young. Later she remarked— "It is impossible that the child of so many prayers could ever perish."

Final thought: Observing and correcting children's lives is no easy task, but Christian parents exist for just this purpose!

Day 116

PROVERBS 20:21

"An inheritance may be gotten hastily at the beginning; but the end thereof shall not be blessed."

Wisdom in Taking Our Time

The old adage "haste makes waste" has a biblical basis! As a general principle, that which comes easily or instantly vanishes just as quickly. Lasting things generally require time and pain to develop. The inheritance that is "gotten hastily" in this verse is obviously that which is gotten by dishonest, manipulative, or selfish means. Its end will not be blessed.

Let this be a warning in the training of children. David calls youth, "an heritage (inheritance) of the Lord" (Ps. 127:3). But such an inheritance is not gained in a day or a year. Rather, true godliness is developed through the slow process of progressive sanctification, and it is the product of an ever-growing relationship with God and obedience to the Word. Manipulation, coercion, and a system of regimented rules may give the illusion of godliness, but "the end thereof shall not be blessed."

It is your mission to begin the process of spiritual growth. You can only do this as you emphasize both the supremacy and the sufficiency of God's Word in the hearts and lives of your children. Only as you confront every area of their life with the question "What does the Bible say?" will the seeds of future godliness be sown!

Final thought: Don't give up! The blessings of the future are sown in the present, and tomorrow's godly leaders often come from unlikely beginnings!

Day 117

"The blueness of a wound cleanseth away evil: so do stripes the inward parts of the belly."

Wisdom in Appropriate Discipline

Punishment is the Lord's way of bringing pain to the flesh to bring profit to the spirit. God's concern is always for the "inward parts." The point of the verse (difficult to accurately translate into proper English), however, seems to be that there are "different strokes for different folks" but always to one end—development of the inner man! The Complete Biblical Library suggests, "The wise understand the need to correct those who are in their care, and to do so thoughtfully, applying the right form of rebuke at the appropriate time (25:11f)."

First Thessalonians 5:14 distinguishes between those who are unruly, feeble-minded, and weak. Each requires a different stroke! The unruly must be *warned* (a Greek word that implies confronting the sinner with Scripture), the feebleminded must be comforted (encouraged), and the weak must be supported. Thus, godly discipline requires discernment, appropriate action, and proper motive.

To discern we must be so transparent with children that they are transparent with us! We must see the mind and heart beyond the action. Only then can we apply appropriate discipline (whether scriptural confrontation, encouragement, or biblical steps for victory). The proper motive is to develop the "inward parts" rather than to simply affect outward change.

Final thought: Without proper medication, wounds are not healed, and without appropriate correction, character is not developed.

Day 118

PROVERBS 21:1

"The king's heart is in the hand of the Lord, as the rivers of water: he turneth it whithersoever he will."

Wisdom in Making an Appeal

What do we do when we disagree with the policies of our child's school or our authorities at work? How do we handle a situation when we want to do something that we think would benefit us (or our children), but those in authority do not agree? We must follow the advice given in this verse.

First, we must recognize that the God who formed the rivers and changes their course as He wills also holds the hearts of those for whom we work or those who teach our children in school in the palms of His hands! He can as easily change the minds of the authorities in our lives as He can change the flow of a mighty river.

Next, armed with that understanding, we go to the King of Kings and ask Him to change the heart of our "king." As we pray, we must also submit ourselves to accept the outcome, whatever it may be. Keep in mind that God works in the heart of the obstinate, the unsaved, and the stubborn, as easily as he works in the heart of the humble, godly leader. No matter how impossible a situation may seem God is able to change the heart of the king!

Finally, appeal to the authority—but only when you have a well thought through (and prayed through) plan to present and a willingness to accept the decision (no matter what it is) as from the Lord.

By the way, a wise parent will teach their child to follow these steps.

Final thought: God can also change your heart and make it willing to accept a contrary decision from your authority.

Day 119

PROVERBS 21:5

"The thoughts of the diligent tend only to plenteousness; but of every one that is hasty only to want."

Wisdom in Plodding

The tortoise wins again! Usually the diligent is contrasted with the lazy. But here, the diligent is contrasted with the hasty. That is, the plodding, thinking, planning, patient, hard-working man makes progress by degrees and ultimately ends up ahead. The hasty are often characterized by undisciplined impulse. They rush ahead without thinking. The mouth moves before the mind is engaged. The hand acts before the heart controls. They are more concerned with saying what they think than with helping their child to understand Biblical truth.

A wise man gave this advice to those who were in a hurry to get things done: "Slow down a little, so we can get this job done sooner!" A diligent parent slows down his life so as to have quality teaching time with his children. He slows down that his children may grow faster. He knows that his children need him more than the money his busy life provides.

The problem with haste in our life is that we have no time for prayer! The problem with haste in our home is that we have little time for our children. The problem with haste in our decisions is that we run ahead of God. The Lord takes His time. He operates from the perspective of eternity, while we operate from the perspective of 70 years! The God of Eternity is our employer, and we must operate by His time card!

Final thought: Haste may waste a heart—your child's!

Day 120

PROVERBS 21:19

"It is better to dwell in the wilderness, than with a contentious and an angry woman."

Wisdom in Controlling Anger

Nothing is as destructive as a quarrelling, angry spouse or parent! Solomon feels so strongly about it that he mentions it again in Proverbs 19:13; 21:9; 25:24; and 27:15. An uncontrolled temper may drive a spouse out of the house! Worse, it may chase children from the home. Contentious, nagging people can so destroy the peace that the goal becomes singular—escape from their presence.

A parent with uncontrolled anger will drive his child to despair. Escape becomes the only hope for the child. How do they escape? Early in life they clam up. As a turtle retreats into his shell, children find shelter in silence. As Cain's anger led to the murder of Abel, so our anger may kill the transparency of open communication in our home. As children grow older, they stay away from home. The mall, their friends (even the wrong kind), and the car become the "wilderness," which is better than their home.

The problem with anger is that everyone but the guilty can see it. It is so much a part of his character that what he calls, "raising my voice a bit" is in reality screaming or shouting. What he calls "telling the truth" is in reality bludgeoning others with hurtful words that cut to the soul. What he calls "discipline" is in reality "undisciplined discipline."

Final thought: Check your Anger Barometer. Do your children openly share their hurts, problems, and prayer requests with you, or do they seek out others? Do they love to be around you, or do they remain aloof?

Day 121

"He that followeth after righteousness and mercy findeth life, righteousness, and honour."

Wisdom in Righteous Pursuits

Twenty-first century life is so fast that even the most committed Christian often struggles with vain priorities. Solomon wrote an entire book on the vanity of wrong pursuits. He called it chasing the wind (Eccles. 5:16).

If mature adults battle with such vanities, our youth struggle all the more. Satan has them chasing soap bubbles. And sadly, they are often led in their empty pursuit by Christian parents and teachers also chasing the wind! How do we make sure our children do not get caught up in such vain pursuits?

First, we must make sure our own pursuits are righteous! Are we most animated when talking of our devotions, of our Lord, of the Word—or when we speak of entertainment, sports, our hobbies, or other pursuits? What kind of example do we set before our children? On what pursuits do they see us spending the most of our time, our energy, and our thought?

Second, we must make sure our righteous pursuits are contagious. This is accomplished by the verbal, enthusiastic sharing of the treasures we glean from our devotions. Your children must hear you talk excitedly about your relationship to the Lord each day.

Finally, share illustrations of the emptiness of chasing the wind. Your newspapers abound with stories of entertainers who chased the wind only to find death from drugs, AIDS, or suicide. Point out the fallacy of such pursuits while watching TV with your child or while reading a book to them. Drawing illustrations from your own life may be most effective.

Final thought: Our hunger for righteousness must be so contagious that our children become Son-chasers rather than wind-chasers.

Day 122

PROVERBS 21:31

"The horse is prepared against the day of battle: but safety is of the Lord."

Wisdom in Preparation

Our children daily go forth to war! Whether they are aware of it or not, they are in a battle with the world, the flesh, and the devil. Billboards, TV, video games, peer pressure, music, and a thousand other things will press the philosophies of the world upon them. To win the battle, they must be adequately prepared. That's where parents come in!

Parents, however, often neglect this important aspect of preparation. We prepare our children for the future with savings accounts and investments. We prepare them for emergencies with insurance. We prepare them for the start of school. We help them in sports or in preparation for a test. But do we prepare them for the most important battle—spiritual warfare?

One aspect of preparation that often goes unnoticed is prayer. Yet, it is probably the most important aspect of preparation. How often do we pray for our children? How often do we stop and ask God for wisdom and insight.

The last phrase of Proverbs 21:31 reminds us that all our preparation is in vain if the Lord is not involved, for "safety is of the Lord." All of our burdens for youth, our words, our urging, our counseling, our discipline, and our teaching are in vain unless the Lord is at work! He is the One whose power must be invoked. The best teaching and urging will fall on deaf ears unless the Lord works in their heart.

Do we depend on our instincts born of years of experience and our authority as parents to make them conform, or do we go forth with trembling and in the power of the Lord, realizing that only He can change their heart?

Final thought: Our most effective preparation of our children is done on our knees!

Day 123

PROVERBS 22:2
"The rich and poor meet together: the Lord is the maker of them all."

Wisdom in Accepting Others

Children struggle with wrong values. In elementary school name-calling and insults are not uncommon. The handicapped, the slow-learner, and the less developed are the objects of cruel jokes. In high school the athletic, the best looking, or the best dressed often lead the popularity parade. Even parents and teachers are often guilty of favoring the exceptional child. It is your task to teach your child to look upon every person equally as the creation of God.

The problem with such cruel behavior is a failure to see people as God sees them. Solomon reminds us that we are all the creation of God. Wealth, poverty, personality, academic, and athletic skills are by God's design. To favor one over the other is to disregard God's design and providence. When children mock another, they mock their Maker (Prov. 14:31; 17:5). Likewise, 1 Corinthians 8:12 reminds us that when we sin against another Christian we "sin against God." These truths should be urged upon your children when you see their mistreatment or favoring of a sibling or another child.

James reminds us of the other side of the coin (2:1–9)—honoring others for their station in life. When we give preferential treatment to those who are more popular, better looking, or better students, we also mock God. Job declared: "For I know not to give flattering titles; in so doing my maker would soon take me away" (Job 32:22). Watch carefully for this trait in your child. Show them that inward character is more important than outward appearance.

Final thought: Right values are the product of a right perspective. Teach your child to see others as God sees them, not looking on the external appearance.

Day 124

PROVERBS 22:3

"A prudent man foreseeth the evil, and hideth himself: but the simple pass on, and are punished."

Wisdom in Foreseeing Future Sin

It is a great part of wisdom to see what God is about to do. When evil comes, most men see it, but the wise foresee it.

Two thoughts emerge from this verse: the necessity of foreseeing evil and the wisdom of fleeing evil. Because youth have problems with the first, they often fall prey to the second—"the simple (naïve, immature) pass on, and are punished."

Wise parents will foresee the adult in the child! They will see the seed of childish temper wrecking a future marriage. They will see the tendency to laziness full-blown in a wasted life. They will see the argumentative spirit leading to an insubordinate employee. They will make the child aware of the future consequences of his childish sins and show him the scriptural steps to correction thereby enabling him to "hide himself" from the evil.

The simple parent will pay little attention to such childish sins, and, thus, the child will pass on to adulthood and face the evils of his sin. Other parents will wring their hands, chastise, or punish the child but fail to offer scriptural correction. Thus, they allow the simple to "pass on" to punishment.

Final thought: Children are too simple to see their sin full-grown. We must foresee it for them and give them corrective steps to hide from the evil.

Day 125

PROVERBS 22:6
"Train up a child in the way he should go: and when he is old, he will not depart from it."

Wisdom in Dedicating Our Children

Entire books have been written on this verse as it relates to parents and teachers. The key to the verse lies in understanding the meaning of *train*. The Hebrew means "to initiate, to begin." Its primary use was in the construction of a building. Its secondary use involved the dedication of a building (e.g., the dedication of Solomon's Temple, 1 Kings 8:63; 2 Chron. 7:5). Thus, the word conveys several key truths for the Christian home. Christian parents initiate the process of building a life that is dedicated to the Lord.

The phrase *in the way he should go* is literally "according to his way." This most likely refers to God's way of wisdom, as opposed to man going his own way (Isa. 53:6). This is in keeping with the primary emphasis of Proverbs, which is submission to the Lord and to His way.

Biblical training (parenting) begins with dedication. The process of training your children begins with dedicating them individually to the Lord. Nothing is more important for both the child and the parent's attitude toward that child. You are training children to be servants of the Lord, not to be better citizens. If your mind and motives have not taken hold of this principle, you will be a misguided parent! Your job is to prepare your children for God's work, not for a secular job! Parental training begins by giving your children to the Lord for His service even as Hanna surrendered Samuel to God.

Final thought: Wise parents dedicate their children to be servants of the Lord.

Day 126

PROVERBS 22:6

"Train up a child in the way he should go: and when he is old, he will not depart from it."

Wisdom in Discipling

Parents are "disciplers." They must do more than teach their children; they must train them. This training is often referred to as discipleship. The concept is found in Matthew 28:19: "Go ye therefore and teach all nations…." The word *teach* is literally "make disciples of." The Great Commission is a call to make disciples not simply to preach the gospel or to teach facts. A parent's responsibility to fulfill the Great Commission must begin with his children.

Discipling in Hebrew and Greek cultures implied both telling and showing—with the emphasis on showing. The master lived with his disciples. Thus, the master's life, spirit, and attitude were as important as the words he spoke. Today, much of that concept has been lost. Parents may verbally disseminate information but are often too busy to get intimately involved in their children's lives. Thus, there is little emphasis on modeling truth in the training process. Parents are too preoccupied with their careers, their burdens, or their hobbies to spend quality time discipling their children! They send them to school and to church in the hope that others will train them.

Training however, involves three levels of learning: the what, the how, and the why. The what teaches facts, the how demonstrates (models) the facts in life situations, and the why emphasizes comprehension. Others may teach them the what, but the how is primarily modeled by parents. If our children do not see the how of Christianity modeled in the life of their parents, they will fail to comprehend the why. Christianity will become little more than creed to be believed and have little impact on how they live.

Final thought: Christian parents have a higher calling than just talking: we are called to model the truth before our children!

Day 127

"Train up a child in the way he should go: and when he is old, he will not depart from it."

Wisdom in Demonstrating Truth

A godly parent teaches not only the what but also the how. Proverbs 22:6 admonishes us to train children in the way they should go (the how). Such teaching emphasizes demonstration both in the laboratory and in life. Which is better—to tell children how to solve a Rubik's cube without trying it, or to give them a Rubik's cube and ask them to solve it? Obviously, the hands-on approach is better. So it is in every aspect of disciple making. Youth may learn facts from their parents lectures, but they learn their values, morals, priorities, and attitudes from those with whom they interact. It is in real life demonstration that you will most effectively teach your children.

Who is training your child? Youth often spend more time with their peers or in front of a TV screen than with their parents! Thus, while parents lecture, peers and a worldly media demonstrate.

It is noteworthy that Christ taught while walking, sitting, eating, or even riding in a boat. He used current situations, interruptions, and occasions to teach truth. Stones, mustard seeds, barley, fishing nets, fig trees—whatever was at hand—became objects to demonstrate biblical truth. But most importantly, He taught by the demonstration of His life! Years later John wrote of, "That which we have…seen…and our hands have handled…" (1 John 1:1). It was the informal interaction with their Master that forever transformed the disciples of Christ.

Final thought: The best lecture is often spoken by our lives and taught by interaction with our children in daily situations.

Day 128

PROVERBS 22:9

"He that hath a bountiful eye shall be blessed; for he giveth of his bread to the poor."

Wisdom in Teaching Charity

Children are selfish by nature. Early on they horde their toys when another child enters the home. Such is the fallen nature of man. They do not have a bountiful eye but a selfish eye.

It is the parent's task to change the heart—and thus the eye! By the age of three children become conscious of emotions in others. They begin to comprehend sadness or joy in the face of mom and may inquire why she is sad. Thus, parents are urged to start teaching charity to their children at this early age.

How do we teach selflessness to a self-filled child? First, we teach by demonstration. We perform acts of mercy and take our child with us as soon as they are old enough to comprehend. Always remember that God's standard is sacrifice, not convenience. If we live by the rule of convenience, our children will likewise become self-centered. When we go to church only when it is convenient, we teach our children to live for self. When we fail to give faithfully to the church, we teach our children that God has little right to their possessions.

Second, we must teach them the Lordship of Christ. We own nothing! Our toys, our homes, our clothes, our money, even our bodies belong to the Lord. They are not ours to horde and lavish for self-gratification. Rather, all things are His and are loaned to us as instruments to use in serving Him! When children see dad using his car to take others to church "because it belongs to God," when they are taught to give a portion of their allowance each Sunday "because it is His," when they help mom prepare food for a needy person, "because God gave us this to share," then they begin to learn the truth behind charity.

Final thought: Demonstration of the Lordship of Christ over our possessions best fights selfishness in our children.

Day 129

PROVERBS 22:15

"Foolishness is bound in the heart of a child; but the rod of correction shall drive it far from him."

Wisdom in Correction

Children are sinners by birth! "Grandma's angels" have horns rather than wings! We do not have to teach our children to lie, to steal, or to be selfish. These come naturally from a heart that is depraved from birth (Ps. 51:5). The parent who does not come to grips with this reality will pay the consequences in days to come, for "foolishness is bound in the heart of a child." Resistance therefore cannot begin too early.

Note that it is foolishness we must address, not childishness. Charles Bridges quotes an early writer as saying, "A child is to be punished, not for being a child, but for being a wicked child." Sometimes we mistake childishness for foolishness and so punish amiss. Too often, however, we mistake foolishness for childishness and fail to punish. Foolishness is the mighty tendency to evil. It is the very root and essence of sin in a fallen nature, the folly of turning away from a God of love. It includes lying, deceit (Ps. 58:3), willfulness, perverseness, and lack of submission to authority (Job 11:12). While we can delight in our children's harmless play, we must never excuse his foolishness with remarks like, "Oh, he's just a child," or "Children will be children, you know!"

The prescribed remedy to the evil that is bound in our children's hearts is clear. Bridges says, "It is vain to bid the sin depart" because "there's very little inclination in the child himself to remove it from him." Rather, "the rod of correction" is distinctly named and repeatedly urged as God's means of cleansing the evil (Prov. 19:18; 23:13–14; 29:17).

Final thought: The best antidote for the poison of sin is the rod of correction.

Day 130

PROVERBS 22:15

"Foolishness is bound in the heart of a child; but the rod of correction shall drive it far from him."

Wisdom in Correcting Children

Parents may punish in anger or they may correct—only the latter is biblical. Solomon encourages the rod of correction, not the rod of wrath. The purpose of correction is exactly that—to correct. Never use times of correction to vent your anger or to show how much you dislike an action.

Love is the ruling principle in the rod of correction. A wise parent will use God's rod to remove men from sin. Hebrews says we discipline not for our pleasure, but for our child's profit, not from whim or passion, but from love for his soul (Heb. 12:10).

When disciplining your child:
- Tell them you do so because you love them.
- Tell them you do so for their benefit.
- Let them know it breaks your heart to discipline but that you do so in obedience to the Lord.
- Discipline them calmly, with a broken heart.

After administering the discipline, put your arm around them and pray with them. Reassure them that you love them and ask God to help them grow up to love and to serve Him.

If a child is punished for falsehood, to avoid future punishment, he abstains and speaks the truth. As he grows, he finds the blessing and comfort of the right path. He learns gradually to speak truth from a higher motive. Insensibly his conscience acquires tenderness in regard to it, and it becomes a principle in his character. In that way, the rod of discipline performs its work with permanent benefit.

Final thought: The rod of correction is designed to correct not to punish.

Day 131

PROVERBS 22:28
"Remove not the ancient landmark, which thy fathers have set."

Wisdom in Staying the Course

Ancient cultures recognized the sacredness of the boundary. Even heathen cultures honored the dividing stone as a god not to be touched. Israel's concept of boundaries came from the conviction that God Himself set the bounds of nations and therefore man must not tamper with them. Thus, "Remove not the ancient landmark (boundary markers), which thy fathers have set."

The home also has divinely established boundaries. We move those boundaries at the risk of destroying our family! Sadly, humanistic thought often enters the doors of our home. We replace Biblical instruction with human reasoning. We sweat with them over their homework and grades but seldom ask them about their devotional and prayer life. We rush them to sports activities but seldom encourage them to Scripture memory and other spiritual exercises that profit for the rest of their lives. We have been fooled into believing that discipline is abusive and will drive our children from us, so we talk to them but seldom admonish. We educate their head but forget their heart. We offer them material things but deprive them of ourselves. In essence, we have moved the ancient landmarks.

Deuteronomy 6:1–9 establishes God's boundaries for parents.

1. Parents must passionately and transparently love the Lord (v. 5).
2. The Word must saturate and grip the father's heart (v. 6).
3. Mom and dad must disciple children by modeling truth in every aspect of daily life (v. 7).

Final thought: Don't move family landmarks: heart over head, relationship over ritual, consecration over conformity, spirituality over sports, godliness over grades, and attitude over academics!

Day 132

PROVERBS 23:15
"My son, if thine heart be wise, my heart shall rejoice, even mine."

Wisdom in Aiming for the Heart

What brings you the most joy in parenting? Is it the changing diapers? Is it correcting your child? Is it cleaning up after them? Is it rising early and going to be late to provide for them? Let's look at what gave Solomon joy.

Solomon focused on his child's heart, not his head ("if thine heart be wise…")! His heart was not that his child would become a great warrior or that he would be successful. His burden was that his child's heart would be wise in the things of God. Undoubtedly, he had learned this from his father. In David's old age he challenged Solomon: "And thou, Solomon, my son, know thou the God of thy father, and serve him with a perfect heart and with a willing mind: for the Lord searcheth all hearts…if thou seek him, he will be found of thee…" (1 Chron. 28:9).

Parents must aim for the heart. An intelligent mind is wasted if the heart is unwise. An athletic body is wasted if the heart is not strong toward God. A skilled musician plays in the minor key if the heart is not in tune with God. God searches the heart of man (1 Sam. 16:7), not the head, not the athletic body, nor the skilled fingers.

What brings you the most joy in parenting? Is it to see your child's heart tender to the things of God, even if she isn't the best student? Is it his heart that thrills us most or the progress he makes in sports or some other talent? Obviously, we want the mind, the talent, and the heart to be surrendered to the Lord. But true godliness begins in the heart.

Final thought: The aim of a wise parent's heart is to aim for the heart of their child.

Day 133

PROVERBS 23:23

"Buy the truth, and sell it not; also wisdom, and instruction, and understanding."

Wisdom in Appreciating Truth

This passage underscores the value of truth. It is worth buying; it is too valuable to sell! Truth is worth any cost, and nothing can replace its loss.

But what is truth? Pilate ironically asked that question of Jesus who had told His disciples, "I am…the Truth" (John 14:6). Truth is all that concerns Jesus Christ our Lord. Truth is accepting Him as our personal Lord and Savior and striving to be conformed to His image. All else is but a mirage.

Biblical parenting seeks to change youth's values. It must escalate the value of obedience to God's Word and expose the high cost of disobedience. He is not educated, though valedictorian, that is not committed to Christ. She is not wise that reads great books but does not know the Book. He is not intelligent that makes straight A's but fails with God!

"Sell it not" brings to mind those who sell the Lord for popularity or career advancement. They compromise truth to fulfill their lusts. Parents must emphasize the value of obedience to God's Word and the cost of disobedience. Many proverbs teach the blessings of wisdom and the folly of disobedience. The appendix contains a list of verses you can use in counseling with your children.

Final thought: Proverbs were written to change youthful values. Use them!

Day 134

PROVERBS 23:26

"My son, give me thine heart, and let thine eyes observe my ways."

Wisdom in Giving Our Heart to God

If you would be a godly parent, give your heart to God! "Oh, but I gave my heart to the Lord when I was saved," you may say. Salvation is only the first step in giving our heart to Him. Solomon has a further step in mind in this passage. You must empty your heart of all that keeps your mind off Him and then fill your heart with thoughts of His glory.

Deuteronomy 6:4–6 reflects this idea: "These words that I command thee this day, shall be in thine heart, and thou shalt teach them diligently to thy children." The principle is clear: A God-focused heart precedes effective parental instruction.

How do we fill our hearts with God? We fill our hearts with Him by filling our eyes with His ways ("and let thine eyes observe my ways"). We do this by reading His Word with an eye toward noting how God operates. *Observing* in the Hebrew means "pleasure, delight, or pleasing." We are to delight in His ways. We must take pleasure in noticing how God operates in given situations. A wise parent will fill his eyes with God's ways and keep a "How God Works" notebook to record his observations. His God-focused eyes will result in a God-focused heart. Nothing is more vital. Give your heart over to God by filling your mind with Him!

Final thought: A God-focused heart precedes a God-focused home.

Day 135

PROVERBS 24:13-14

"My son, eat thou honey, because it is good; and the honeycomb, which is sweet to thy taste: So shall the knowledge of wisdom be unto thy soul: when thou hast found it, then there shall be a reward, and thy expectation shall not be cut off."

Wisdom in Feeding Our Minds

Nothing is sweeter than honey. We eat it with delight. Such is the sweetness of God's Word. Like the honeycomb, it is delightful and energizing to the godly. David calls God's Word sweeter than the honeycomb (Ps. 19:10), and again "sweeter than honey to my mouth" (Ps. 119:103).

But the sweetness of God's Word is an acquired taste! Hebrews 5:14 reminds us that the enjoyment of God's Word belongs to those "that are of full age, even those who by reason of use have their senses exercised to discern both good and evil." In other words, God's Word is not as tasty to some as to others. What makes it sweeter to some? The continual use and exercise of the Word makes it sweeter. Daily, habitual meditation on God in the Word improves with use! At first the believer finds it difficult to understand and enjoy (Ps. 119:25–28). But eventually he can say, "How sweet are thy words to my taste" (Ps. 119:103).

The sweetness of the Word will bring sweetness to our home. The father who is full of the glory of God will not speak like the man who is drunk—whether it be with alcohol or pride. The dad who is filled with God's Word will use the rod of correction rather than the rod of anger. The mother who is filled with the Spirit will bring a sweet spirit of joy to the home rather than a dark cloud of weariness.

Finally, the family that feeds on the sweetness of Christ shall be rewarded ("there shall be a reward"). God will pour His blessing upon both parents and children. Their "expectation shall not be cut off." That is, their hopes shall be realized and God will do "exceeding abundantly above all that we ask or think." Should this not be motivation enough to spend more time tasting His sweetness in the Word?

Final thought: A parent is not spiritually fit until his soul delights in the sweetness of God's Word.

Day 136

PROVERBS 24:13-14

"My son, eat thou honey, because it is good; and the honeycomb, which is sweet to thy taste: So shall the knowledge of wisdom be unto thy soul: when thou hast found it, then there shall be a reward, and thy expectation shall not be cut off."

Wisdom in Discovering God's Word

What is the sweetness of wisdom described in this passage? I suggest two things: 1) the sweetness of God's Person that permeates His Word and 2) the sweetness of discovery!

As to the sweetness of God's Person, we must realize that His Word was given to reveal Him! If we only see facts, stories, and information in His Word, we see little more than the unsaved. Believers, however, should see God's glorious character in every verse and passage. The wise reader will learn to focus on God in the Word, rather than focus on the Word of God!

As to the sweetness of discovery, we will be blessed "when thou hast found it." What is it that is found? Is it not when our eyes discover a truth we had not seen before? Is it not when what once looked like a single grain of truth, opens to become a field of waving barley? Is it not when we begin to see glimpses of His glory in every passage we read? Ah, this is true sweetness! As the gold miner cries "Eureka," when he strikes a vein of gold, so we cry "Hallelujah" when our once dull eyes glimpse His glory in the Word!

Final thought: If you struggle in the Word, keep digging. By "reason of use" you will soon discover the sweetness of His Word!

Day 137

PROVERBS 24:16

"For a just man falleth seven times, and riseth up again: but the wicked shall fall into mischief."

Wisdom in Handling the Easily Discouraged

Not all rebels are rebels! As we have noted previously, 1 Thessalonians 5:14 describes three types of problem youth: the rebel, the easily discouraged, and the weak (the unruly, feebleminded, and weak). All may appear to be rebellious, but that's only an outward facade. The easily discouraged may slump in his seat, mumble when he talks, pay little attention when dad speaks, or fail to do his work. However, his heart—unlike the rebellious—wants to do right, but he thinks he can't! The easily discouraged give up easily. Some are perfectionists and would rather do nothing than try and fail. Others are insecure and lack the confidence to try. Either way they are defeated by defeat. If they once fail, they quit. They need encouragement, not criticism. The parent who treats the easily discouraged as though he was a rebel only discourages him the more.

Instead, have him memorize this verse. Show him that even the great Michael Jordan would sometimes fall down on the court, but he didn't lie there. He got up and tried again. Challenge him to get up—to claim this verse—and to go out and try it again! Only the wicked *fall* into mischief. This is a different Hebrew word from falleth in the beginning of the verse. This word means to fall due to a physical condition (i.e., their rebellious heart). They don't get up because they are spiritually dead.

Final thought: Both the just and the wicked will fall. The difference is found in who gets up!

Day 138

PROVERBS 24:27

"Prepare thy work without, and make it fit for thyself in the field; and afterwards build thine house."

Wisdom in Preparation

Youth often want the house without the work! They want good grades without studying. They want to succeed without discipline and sweat. This verse reminds us that before the house comes the work. There must be preparation in the street ("prepare thy work without") and making ready the field before one can build the house. Nice homes and cars are the result of long years of diligent work. The things adults enjoy are due to sacrifice and sweat, not the lottery! This is a difficult lesson for youth who live in a get-rich-quick society.

Parents must learn this lesson as well. If youth are houses, we build them through careful preparation. Godly children are the result of prayer, filling our heart with the Word, deepening our relationship with the Lord, and using the Word to counsel them. Christian homes don't automatically produce godly youth. They are the result of diligent heart preparation by dedicated parents with one goal—the godliness of the child. Sadly, some spend more time in food preparation than in heart preparation! They spend more time fixing their face than filling their heart.

Parents often exercise greater care in their child's academic preparation than in their heart preparation because they are more focused on students' grades than their godliness. Grades may be important, but godliness is profitable for all things. God used both Paul the scholar and Peter the uneducated fisherman, but the common thread in both was the golden thread of godliness. In all your preparation, prepare your heart and that of your child!

Final thought: Before we build godly youth, we must prepare the field of our heart.

Day 139

PROVERBS 24:33-34

"Yet a little sleep, a little slumber, a little folding of the hands to sleep: So shall thy poverty come as one that travelleth; and thy want as an armed man."

Wisdom in Redeeming the Time

Charles Spurgeon is our teacher today. Let's read what he has to say about the sluggard:

"The worst of sluggards only ask for a little slumber; they would be indignant if they were accused of thorough idleness…. Yet by littles the day ebbs out, and the time for labour is all gone, and the field is grown over with thorns. It is by little procrastinations that men ruin their souls. They have no intention to delay for years—a few months will bring the more convenient season—tomorrow if you will, they will attend to serious things; but the present hour is so occupied and altogether so unsuitable, that they beg to be excused. Like sands from an hourglass, time passes, life is wasted by driblets, and seasons of grace lost by little slumbers. Oh, to be wise, to catch the flying hour, to use the moments on the wing."

Such were men's thoughts at the close of the 19th Century. If it was so then, it is more so now! A century has brought more ease and entertainment to distract from the urgency of the hour. Yet, are we not nearer the final days than then? Satan would steal the hearts of our youth. It is "high time to awake out of sleep: for now is our salvation nearer than when we believed" (Rom. 13:11). The enemy of idleness is at the door to steal the hearts of our youth.

Parents wake up too late and find the days are gone. Their children are grown, and with alarm they realize they let time slip by, always planning to spend more time with them tomorrow. But tomorrow was always the next day or the next week. The harvest passed, and the crop was left to rot in the field.

Final thought: Carpe diem—seize the day lest the enemy seize our youth!

Day 140

PROVERBS 25:2

"It is the glory of God to conceal a thing: but the honour of kings is to search out a matter."

Wisdom in Searching God's Glory

God's glory is unfathomable. What glory could belong to a god whose name, ways, and works could be fully understood by mortal man? We look at His ways and discover "Thy way is in the sea, and thy path in the great waters, and thy footsteps are not known" (Ps. 77:19). We view His forgiveness and realize that no human wisdom can understand the full extent of His grace. We view His work in creation and salvation and proclaim, "O the depth of the riches both of the wisdom and knowledge of God! How unsearchable are his judgments, and his ways past finding out" (Rom. 11:33). Charles Bridges asked, "Are not the clouds of His concealment the brightness of His glory?"

By contrast, the glory of kings is to search out knowledge! We know nothing compared to the vast universe of God's knowledge. It is our glory to spend our days searching out the "unsearchable riches of Christ" (Eph. 3:8). But though we spend our lifetime in searching out His glory in all we see, we would catch but a glimpse of the edge of His brightness. For who could see His full brightness (Exo. 33:20–23) who "dwelleth in the light which no man can approach unto" (1 Tim. 6:16)?

Final thought: The glory of your life is to reveal His glory in your dealings with your child. He is there. Search Him out and reveal Him to your children!

Day 141

PROVERBS 25:2

"It is the glory of God to conceal a thing: but the honour of kings is to search out a matter."

Wisdom in a Leaf, Part 1

Some things are too small to be seen; others are too large. Can we with the naked eye see the tiny atom or the far reaches of the universe? One is too minute to be seen and the other is too vast—yet in both the glory of God is concealed. It is man's glory to search out the King's glory in all of His creation. Over the next three days we will search out His glory in a leaf! As a parent you often have the opportunity to point out God's glory in nature. The next three days will provide an exercise for doing just that. Read the following paragraph and record on the next page what you see of God's glory from the tiny leaf.

We could not live without leaves! They are amazing solar factories that manufacture food for plants. Without this food, plants could not live. Without plants, animals and humans could not live. Leaves provide man with shade, oxygen, and moisture (an Elm transpires one ton of water a day into our atmosphere), and they beautify the earth. The largest leaf is the South American Palm, measuring 26' x 5'. The smallest is the Wolfie, which gives ponds their greenish tint. The most numerous leaf is the Diatom (invisible without a microscope). They are found in every drop of water on the surface of oceans, and they provide 90% of the food for fish. Each is a beautiful work of art with hard transparent crystal covers marked with beautiful variegated colors. There are billions of oak leaves, but no two are identical! Every leaf is comprised of three main parts: a blade, a stem, and a stipule.

Final thought: If God's glory is concealed in a leaf, what must be in the sun!

God's Glory in a Leaf, Part 1

Record your thoughts from today on the lines below.

Day 142

"It is the glory of God to conceal a thing: but the honour of kings is to search out a matter."

Wisdom in a Leaf, Part 2

God's glory is inexhaustible. It is in all we see yet we often overlook it! The angels declared: "Holy, holy, holy, is the LORD of hosts: the whole earth is full of his glory." The universe is but a giant theater to reveal the concealed glory of God. It is our glory (i.e., the greatest thing we can do) to search it out and share His glory with others. Let's continue searching out His glory in a tiny leaf. Read the following paragraphs and continue to record the things you see of His glory on the page provided.

Each leaf is like a room. It has a floor and a roof supported by thousands of tiny pillars. Inside this room food is manufactured. Sunlight filters through the transparent roof above. The floor below has up to 100,000 stomata (mouths) per inch that open and close to let in air. Two "guards" stand at each stomata to see that the right amount of oxygen and water enter the room.

The pillars (palisades) are covered with green chemical specks which we call chlorophyll. The filtered sun strikes the chlorophyll initiating a chemical reaction called photosynthesis. Carbon and other elements of the air entering through the stomata change to starch, sugar, and oil, resulting in the production of food!

It takes twelve banana leaves to produce sixty pounds of bananas, fifteen leaves to produce a cluster of grapes, thirty leaves to produce a peach, and fifty leaves to make an apple!

Final thought: Good parents are glory-miners, digging out God's glory in every thing they see and sharing it with their children! What riches have you mined today?

God's Glory in a Leaf, Part 2

Record your thoughts from today on the lines below.

Day 143

PROVERBS 25:2

"It is the glory of God to conceal a thing: but the honour of kings is to search out a matter."

Wisdom in a Leaf, Part 3

It has been our glory to search out His glory in a tiny leaf. The purpose of these three devotionals is to demonstrate how you should show God's glory to your children in every aspect of life and nature. Compare your notes from the past two days with what follows. Perhaps you saw some things not mentioned here. Such is the depth of His glory. Though we plumb the depths or scale the heights for a thousand years, we could but see the corona of His glory! Notice God's glory in the leaf:

- His infinite wisdom—Which of us could have thought of such a thing when it did not exist?
- His perfect order and design—God created the amazing symmetry and efficiency of a solar unit by placing the smallest solar factory known to man inside the leaf.
- His infinite knowledge—He knows everything about our solar power, even things we are only now discovering.
- His care and provision for man—He provides us with shade, beauty, and food through a leaf, displaying His concern for us.
- His infinite detail—His attention to minute details of design are seen in the stomata, the palisades, the transparent roof, and the little guards that regulate the intake of oxygen and water.
- His omnipotence—God's power is seen in the power to make such a machine and in the power of that machine to make food.
- His efficiency—In the leaf, nothing is wasted. Even dying leaves provide beauty, enrich the soil, and provide much needed exercise for man in raking them.

Final thought: Psalm 104:24, "O Lord, how manifest are thy works! In wisdom hast thou made them all: the earth is full of thy riches."

Day 144

PROVERBS 25:4-5

"Take away the dross from the silver, and there shall come forth a vessel for the finer. Take away the wicked from before the king, and his throne shall be established in righteousness."

Wisdom in Seeing Beyond the Slag

The principle is simple: refining produces silver for the smith. The applications are many:

1. Organizations (national, church, school, business) must purge the wicked from their midst before the Lord will bless (the application Solomon uses here).
2. We must be cleansed of sin to be fit for the Master's use (2 Tim. 2:21).
3. The fires of persecution and trials produce patience, character, and beauty of soul.
4. The refiner (parent) sees past the dross and refines it for the silversmith (the Lord) to work His craft and produce a vessel of beauty and value.

All of these apply to the home. Our children are born in sin, and early on their sin nature is seen. The wise parent looks beyond the dross and sees pure silver in the most insubordinate and least promising child. Godly parents know that even the most mischievous and immature child might be a future servant of the Lord.

But how is the dross removed? First, parents must teach their children the gospel of Christ. They must see His glory in nature and in the Word. Our children need to know the Lord and experience His work of salvation.

Second, children should memorize Scripture. Parents should lead their children to memorize passages that deal with specific sin in their life. "Thy word have I hid in mine heart that I might not sin against thee" (Ps. 119:11).

Finally, children must develop a passion for the Lord. Parents should magnify the majesty of God by teaching their children both the names of God (see list in the appendix) and the attributes of God and by showing their children His majesty in nature. Only as a child is led to admire His glory will they develop a passion for Him. Such love will purge the dross and produce the pure silver (1 Cor. 13).

Final thought: Beyond the dross is silver God can use. It is your job to refine it!

Day 145

PROVERBS 25:11
"A word fitly spoken is like apples of gold in pictures of silver."

Wisdom in Gracious Speech

Apples of gold resting in baskets of silver filigree—such is the picture Solomon uses of proper speech. The allusion teaches us much about the speech of the wise.

First, our speech must be "fitly spoken." That is, it must be appropriate for the moment—words that fit the occasion. Job declares, "How forcible are right words" (Job 6:25). Our Lord Himself was concerned with right words for the right moment, saying that the Father hath "given me the tongue of the learned, that I should know how to speak a word in season to him that is weary" (Isa. 50:4). Rotten apples in silver filigree baskets are a disgrace. Choose your words well. They must be used in good taste—with decorum, control, and grace.

Fitly spoken is literally "words upon the wheels," that is, words that flow naturally, unforced, rolling smoothly from the occasion. Christ's discourses on the living water and the bread of life arose naturally out of conversation, making them much more powerful.

Words upon the wheels also implies planned speech. Unsavory fruit is placed in the basket when we speak by impulse and irritation.

Finally, speaking upon the wheels indicates repetition. Solomon himself repeats similar proverbs to the slothful, the scorner, and the fool. As wagon wheels running over the same ground create a path, so thoughts revisited stick in the mind.

Final thought: Golden apples grow on cultivated trees. Fill your mind with God's Word if you would fill your mouth with His words.

Day 146

"He that hath no rule over his own spirit is like a city that is broken down, and without walls."

Wisdom in Self-Control

The easiest way for Satan to enter a home is through the loss of self-control! Every fit of uncontrolled anger breaches the walls of our spirit and allows the enemy to gain entrance. Once he breaches the walls, the angry soul fires unfit words in every direction like hot arrows "as a madman who casteth firebrands, arrows, and death" (Prov. 26:18). He is careless of who gets hit or hurt. His words cut deep, and even the innocent are wounded. Thus, the parent who cannot control his spirit wounds his home. How opposite the scene of those words are apples of gold in pictures of silver!

How do we maintain our defenses against injurious, angry speech? Charles Bridges speaks of one defense: "Every outbreaking of irritation, every spark of pride kindling in the heart, must be attacked, and determinately resisted. It is the beginning of a breach in the walls of the city. Without instant attention, it will widen to the ruin of the whole…. Effective self-control is divine grace, not one's own native power. What then is to be done? On the first assault fortify the walls by prayer. Trust not in the strength of the citadel."

We may add another line of defense: filling our minds with the Word of God. "Thy word have I hid in mine heart, that I might not sin against thee" (Ps. 119:11). Fortify your mind with verses that deal with the sin of anger and intemperance. God's Word acts as a secondary wall to keep anger from bursting forth in a volcanic explosion of fire and violence.

Final thought: Fits of uncontrolled temper make one unfit to lead his home!

Day 147

PROVERBS 26:1
"As snow in summer, and as rain in harvest, so honor is not seemly for a fool."

Wisdom in Giving Honor

Paul beseeches us to give honor to whom honor is due (Rom. 13:7). Solomon reveals him to whom honor is not due—the fool. There are two main Hebrew words for *fool* in Proverbs—*kesil* and *ewil*. The former comes from a word meaning to be sluggish, fat, or dull. I call him the Pig-headed Fool. He doesn't care what people say or think. He is often lazy, sloppy, and uncaring. The latter term describes someone who is hot-headed and stubborn. I call him the Bull-headed Fool. He rushes in with impulse, temper, and lack of self-control.

In this case, the Pig-headed fool is not to be honored. Here is one who doesn't listen to advice or instruction. You can attempt to teach him something, but it's as though he was never instructed. Stubbornly, dully he plods along, refusing to listen or to care. To honor him is as unfitting as snow in the middle of summer or as a heavy rain that drowns the field at the time of harvest.

The principle is applicable in a Christian school or home. Schools often honor the athlete—even though they may be ungodly in their life—by choosing them as captain, calling on them to pray, naming them the MVP, and so on. Parents, while understandably supporting their child, may leave the impression that everything is fine as long as junior is good in sports or academics. This can be extremely dangerous. We must make certain that we honor obedience to God above all else. Our excitement for our child's spiritual growth should be rewarded far more than his or her other achievement.

Final thought: We dishonor God when we honor the godless—even when they are our own children!

Day 148

PROVERBS 26:13

"The slothful man saith, There is a lion in the way; a lion is in the streets."

Wisdom in Dealing with Excuses

Parents know excuses! They have heard them all. The truth is that most excuses are a cover for laziness. The slothful claims he couldn't do his homework or chores at home because there was a lion in the street.

How must we treat excuses? First, realize that every child is a sinner, and deceit is born in their hearts. The wise parent does not automatically accept excuses, but neither should parents suspect every excuse. There are legitimate reasons that interfere with duties, and parents must be as sensitive to these as they are suspicious of others. Nothing is worse than doubting truth! It sends a signal to the child that you question his character.

Second, see slothfulness behind most lame excuses, and be ready to scripturally deal with it. Use verses such as today's when your child makes up excuses for failure. Show them their real problem, laziness. Call it what God calls it—the sin of slothfulness.

Third, help them overcome their slothfulness. Tell them you want to help them overcome this debilitating sin. Ask them to search Proverbs for every occurrence of the word *slothful* (11 occasions), to write out each verse, and to explain what each means. Use these verses each time they show a slothful tendency. Use Romans 12:11 to reinforce the value of diligence in work.

Finally, be sure to compliment them for the progress they make. Commend them in front of others. Don't leave them with the impression they are a hopeless sloth! An unexpected reward for diligence will bolster future fervency.

Final thought: There is no excuse for laziness.

Day 149

"The sluggard is wiser in his own conceit than seven men that can render a reason."

Wisdom in Overcoming Sluggishness

Once more we meet the lazy man! This is the last of a four-verse stanza on the slothful. As we study Proverbs we see this man often. Evidently, it is a characteristic God despises in a believer. Two Hebrew words are used repeatedly to describe this man. One word means to be slow, idle, and lazy. It describes one who refuses to work (Prov. 6:6–8); who loves excessive sleep (6:9); who makes up excuses for not working (26:13); who is too lazy to eat (19:24; 26:15); who irritates those for whom he works (10:26); and whose fields (i.e., bedroom, house, desk, yard) are unkept and overgrown with weeds and thorns (24:30–34).

The other Hebrew word used for the slothful man means to be slack or negligent. It describes those who do not take pride in their work aiming instead to get by with the least amount of effort.

The problem with both is conceit. He will argue with seven men, wiser than he and not change his ways. He thinks himself a genius and prides himself in how efficiently he avoids work! He has found ways to avoid exertion and doesn't realize that he is lazy! He believes that, in his scant few years of life, he has already accumulated more wisdom and knowledge than mom and dad combined!

Till now we have applied these verses to our children. Let's apply them now to parents! In what respect are we influenced by the conceit of slothfulness? Does it affect our prayer life or yielding to wise counsel? Does it affect the time we spend on our knees or in Bible-reading asking God for wisdom in rearing our children? Do we allow little aches and pains to keep us from faithfulness in church or in performing other family duties while convincing ourselves that it really hurts worse than they do? Our children will often see through such devices and learn the same slothful behavior.

Final thought: Heaven will never be won by folded arms! "The violent take it by force" (Matt. 11:12).

Day 150

PROVERBS 26:18–19

"As a mad man who casteth firebrands, arrows, and death, So is the man that deceiveth his neighbor, and saith, Am not I in sport?"

Wisdom in Sobriety

Youth are often violent. Cruelty flows from their mouth as easily as water over a dam. Little do they realize that the barbs and taunts they throw at those less gifted may be as violent as shooting them with a gun! They are totally unaware of the misery they bring upon others. They often bear no malice but simply don't think. Their buddies laugh with them and join in triumph over the victim. But God describes them as a "mad man" scattering "firebrands, arrows, and death."

When fun is in good taste, it is harmless. However, practical jokes (innocent as they may seem), mockery, or teasing often get out of hand. When the action deceives or wounds its victim going beyond the bounds of godliness, it ceases to be sport. It then becomes violence and a tool for destroying the spirit of the victim!

Parents must be sensitive to this malady among youth. They must not allow their child to laugh at other youth or make jokes about their clumsiness, appearance, or lack of academic ability.

Neither should parents laugh at their children or belittle them, especially in front of others. Mocking children, playing practical jokes on them, or laughing at their failure is devastating to the atmosphere of the home. It is as destructive to the parents' effectiveness as it is demoralizing to the child. The wise parent is thoughtful of her child's feelings and avoids violent words. Matthew Henry warns, "He that sins in jest, must repent in earnest; or his sin will be his ruin."

Final thought: Words can kill.

Day 151

PROVERBS 27:5
"Open rebuke is better than secret love."

Wisdom in Expressing Love

Not everyone knows how to express love. Childhood abuse, lack of outward expressions of love from parents, embarrassment, spurned love, or deep insecurity all may contribute to the concealment of affection. Parents with such backgrounds may love, but they may have difficulty in expressing it. Yet, God says it is better to openly rebuke someone than to love them but never show it.

Parents must be open, transparent, and loving of their children. Did not Jesus openly express His love for us in coming to earth to die for our sins? We may be afraid to express our love for fear of being rejected, but Christ expressed His love though He knew He would be spurned! Such is the kind of love a parent needs for his children. Such love should be expressed daily in both words and deeds.

How do we express our love for our children? We love them first by telling them that we love them! Some children have never heard the three magic words, "I love you," from their parents. We also love them by giving them our time and attention when they speak. We encourage their words and actions with compliments rather than criticism. We tell them how proud we are of them, even when they are not the best in their class. We love our children by giving them ourselves rather than just giving them things.

But we also show our love by rebuking them when they fail. A true friend will not let those he loves fall into hurtful sin or harmful habits. He will love them enough to confront them with Scripture. "Open rebuke is better than secret love."

Final thought: Expressions of love are more important than claims of love. Give your children your attention, your time, your thoughtfulness, your counsel, and, when needed, loving rebuke.

Day 152

"The full soul loatheth an honeycomb; but to the hungry soul every bitter thing is sweet."

Wisdom in Discerning the Hungry Soul

Not every child hungers for spiritual growth! This can be seen in the natural realm. Abundance, instead of increasing happiness, deprives one of joy! Boredom sets in, and apathy follows. Yet, the poor, hungry for the goods of the rich, strive to have what the rich man loathes! Israel, filled with "angel's food," loathed and trod it under foot as "light bread" (Ps. 78:23–32).

Is this not also true in the realm of the spiritual? The Laodicean church "rich and increased with goods" loathed the honeycomb of the Word (Rev. 3:17–18). So are those who have not been born again. They may read the Bible but only because others make them. They may merely read to discover curious facts or even to belittle the precious truths contained in the Word.

Note those moments when your children express hunger or interest in spiritual things and feed them the Bread of Life. You will see their spiritual appetite grow during family devotions or at church. They will be like boys at a picnic: first in line, with fork and plate in hand! In church you will see the hungry child with his Bible open, pen in hand, taking notes, and asking questions after church. When you have family devotions, hungry children will not twiddle their thumbs or yawn while you speak. They will participate with thought and concern. Hungry children meditate, voluntarily pray, keep a prayer list, and sometimes weep for their friends.

Parents, what of your spiritual appetite? Do you long for His Word? Do you have an insatiable hunger to grow? Are even the hard truths of the Word, which convict of sin, sweet to your soul? Do you hungrily glean, even when the preacher gives but the most meager of food? "Blessed are they that hunger and thirst after righteousness, for they shall be filled."

Final thought: Only a hungry parent can produce a hungry child!

Day 153

PROVERBS 27:8
"As a bird that wandereth from her nest, so is a man that wandereth from his place."

Wisdom in Knowing Yourself

As the bird is safest in her nest, so is man safest where he belongs. The problem is that many of us don't know where we belong in life. There are the discontented who wander from one job to another. No place is large enough for their talents. Thus, like the bird who has lost his nest, they flit from one place to another seeking their dream but finding none.

The ambitious father is often full of zeal for self rather than for his family. He has too many important things to do to notice the needs of his children or wife. After all, he has the weight of his career to worry about. He must not be detracted by simple family matters. The mother can take care of domestic things while he fills his place in the business community. But is not this parent wandering from his place? A father's first responsibility is to the family in which God has placed him. The father (or mother) who wraps his life up in his career has "wandered from his place," and this wandering will become evident in his children. Our wisdom is to understand "our own way" (Prov. 16:9) and to do "our own business" (1 Thess. 4:11), and our first business is our family.

The unsteady finds no church sound enough for him. He wanders from church to church until he discovers another inconsistency, and he is away again carrying his weary family with him.

The dreaming parent cannot find his dream. Perhaps he will be this; perhaps he would rather be that. He runs from job to job, while his wife and children suffer from the lack of stability.

The wise know what they can do, what they cannot do, and what they should do. The wise know that God requires but one thing—faithfulness where He has planted them! "Brethren, let every man, wherein he is called, therein abide with God" (1 Cor. 7:24).

Final thought: Stick to the nest in which God has placed you and faithfully tend your flock!

Day 154

PROVERBS 27:17

"Iron sharpeneth iron: so a man sharpeneth the countenance of his friend."

Wisdom in Personalizing Our Parenting, Part 1

Man is made for companionship" (Bridges). Without social interaction we would be miserable. We would lose the ability to communicate. We would lose our motivation for living and our creativity. The collision of minds whets the edges of both as steel sharpens the edge of a knife.

Some of the most valuable discoveries of science are due to teamwork. One has an idea, another has an improvement, and a third adds the final component. There are many examples in the Bible: David had Jonathan, Naomi had Ruth, and Timothy had Paul. Paul was often refreshed by the countenance of his friends (Acts 18:5; 28:14; 2 Cor. 7:6). The Lord sent the disciples out in pairs. The Church was formed on this basis. Thus, we are not to forsake the assembling of ourselves together (Heb. 10:24–25).

Likewise, children need parents who are involved in their lives. They need the camaraderie of their parents in daily situations. Our Lord did not live to Himself, but in the camaraderie of twelve disciples. He was not a loner. He knew that to impact His disciples He must spend time with them. Thus, we find Him eating with them, fishing with them, and traveling in their company. His most fruitful times with His disciples were when He was with His disciples. Likewise, parents must spend time with their children: eating, hiking, camping, playing games, going on trips, getting ice-cream, shopping, and going to church.

Final thought: Your children need you more than they need your words or possessions!

Day 155

PROVERBS 27:19
"As in water face answereth to face, so the heart of man to man."

Wisdom in Personalizing Our Parenting, Part 2

When one looks in water (or in a mirror), he sees a reflection of his own face. Thus, "face answereth to face." Herein is a lesson for parents: head speaks to head. What we know in our head we teach to our children's heads. Information is passed from our head to the head of our children. This is informational instruction, as we have learned in a previous devotional.

The Christian home, however, is interested in heart instruction, and only a heart can teach another heart—"…so the heart of man to man."

If heads teach through words, how do hearts teach? Hearts teach through interpersonal relationships, and hearts learn by observation. Thus, our hearts reach the hearts of our children when we spend time with them. As heads teach facts, so hearts teach values. Someone has said, "Values are caught rather than taught." Heads cannot teach values; that is the job of the heart. As children observe our values, their hearts are affected. As they see our excitement about the Lord, they get excited. It is not enough to tell them to love the Lord. They must see how love for the Lord is lived in the lives of their parents. Sadly, there is often a gap in what parents say with their mouth and what they actually teach with their actions. Yet, it is the actions that mold our youth, not our words!

Two truths are borne out in this verse. First, we must be righteous if we expect our offspring to be righteous. Second, we must spend quality time with our children so they have ample opportunity to see and learn from our righteous hearts. Thus, it behooves us to 1) make sure our hearts are on fire for God and to 2) spend enough time with our children that their hearts catch that fire!

Final thought: Take time to be holy, then spend time with your children!

Day 156

PROVERBS 27:18

"Whoso keepeth the fig tree shall eat the fruit thereof: so he that waiteth on his master shall be honored."

Wisdom in Serving

Parents get discouraged. The pay is not great! They are mostly under-appreciated. Their children think they are dumb, out of touch, and "just don't understand." Parenting is a 24/7 job with no vacation. This verse should give parents great encouragement! The fig tree was a valuable product in Judea (Mic. 4:4; Hab. 3:17; Luke 13:6) that provided nourishment and sustenance in a non-refrigerated world! Yet those who tended the fig were considered lower-class citizens in the eyes of most. Nevertheless, the keeper of the fig tree was recompensed by eating its fruit.

Likewise, parenting is not always looked upon as a glamorous job. Yet, the rewards of faithful parenting far exceed the rewards of the successful businessman who loses his children in his pursuit of wealth. The richest families are those where parents pour their lives and time into the spiritual growth of their children. They will be rewarded with children who love the Lord with all their heart and grow up to call their parents "blessed."

How sad to see wealthy parents with spiritually impoverished children. How poor are those parents. How wonderful to see godly parents with spiritually thriving children. How rich are those parents though they may barely make ends meet! It isn't the size of our income but the spiritual health of our children that determines our wealth!

Eli was a wealthy priest, but his sons brought him disgrace and death. Solomon lived a life of opulence, but his children sought not the God of Israel or of their grandfather David. How much better to take a cut in pay and receive a raise in our families!

Final thought: Our greatest wealth is the spiritual health of our children. Are you investing in the right place?

Day 157

"Be thou diligent to know the state of thy flocks, and look well to thy herds."

Wisdom in Knowing Our Children

Parents, like pastors, are shepherds. Their children are their flock. And, like shepherds, they must be diligent to know the state of each of their sheep. In ancient times, every sheep was precious. It was a grief to lose one to the lion or the bear. So David "fed them according to the integrity of his heart: and guided them by the skillfulness of his hands" (Ps. 78:72). Whether the object of his integrity was the sheep that he led as a youth or the people that he led as an adult, he led them with the same integrity and care.

It is imperative that we so shepherd our children. We must be diligent to know the spiritual state of each child in our care. We look beyond their appearance, their behavior, or their academic and athletic achievements. We consider their heart—whether they are lost or saved, godly or ungodly, caring or uncaring. Though we are concerned for their physical and mental state, we are more concerned for their spiritual depth. We don't just take them to church, send them to a Christian school, or home school them; we observe how much they speak of the things of the Lord. We check to see if they have a desire for devotions. We observe whether they have a tender heart for the Lord, whether they are broken when they sin, and whether they have a willingness to serve Him or a desire to do His will.

Shepherding parents are more concerned for their child's love for God than for his love of sports. They are more concerned for their desire to know the Word than their desire to know the latest movie or the words to the latest rap song.

Do you as diligently check your child's spiritual temperature as you do his report card or his progress in sports? Do you encourage him to have devotions as much as you encourage him to do well in school?

Final thought: How well do you know your child's spiritual temperature? How concerned are you to know that he is growing in the Lord?

Day 158

PROVERBS 28:1

"The wicked flee when no man pursueth; but the righteous are bold as a lion."

Wisdom in Discerning Guilt

Parents must discern sin behind behavior. Children may hide their sin, but it is not as easy to hide their guilt! Often what appears to be fear (fleeing when no one pursues), or lack of confidence, or the inability to concentrate, may be the result of a deeper problem—unconfessed sin. If you deal only with the fruit and fail to discover the root, you will not help your child.

What are the signs of guilt?

- Guilt causes youth to hide from God and God's people (Gen. 3:8; Isa. 2:19; Luke 5:8).
- Guilty youth are uncomfortable around godly people. They do not enjoy prayer, devotional times, or church. They appear to be secretive and devious.
- Guilt diverts the eyes from looking up (Ezra 9:6). Ezra's guilt kept him from looking up at God, and guilty youth often divert their eyes from looking at an authority figure. They would rather look down than up.
- Guilt produces restlessness (Ps. 38:3).
- Guilt often produces uneasiness, anger, and a quick temper in a child.
- Guilt robs one of joy and happiness (Ps. 32:3; 38:4).
- Guilt-ridden youth are sullen; they don't sing; and they would rather smirk than laugh.
- Guilt may produce physical problems (Ps. 32:3–4).
- Guilt causes lack of concentration (Ps. 51:3). Preoccupation with guilt robs a child of the ability to concentrate in school or do his homework.
- Guilt separates from God (Isa. 59:2).
- Guilty youth show little interest in prayer, church, or devotions.

Final thought: Dealing with the fruit but not the root is like putting a band-aid on cancer!

Day 159

PROVERBS 28:1

"The wicked flee when no man pursueth; but the righteous are bold as a lion."

Wisdom in Detecting Innocence

The signs of a righteous person will also help us to detect a guilty person because their characteristics are completely opposite.

- Righteous youth have nothing to hide (they are "bold as a lion") so they are open and transparent. They often "spill their guts" (like a first grader who tells all to the consternation of his parents).
- The Righteous enjoy prayer, Bible study, and devotions. They ask questions, and they get involved (Ps. 140:13).
- Righteous youth are at peace with themselves and everyone else. They have anger under control and enjoy life (Ps. 55:22; 72:7).
- Righteous youth are happy and laugh easily. They sing without shame and are enthusiastic and energetic in activities (Ps. 32:11; 64:10). A sullen attitude is a sure sign of guilt, not righteousness.
- Righteous youth have a better ability to concentrate because their mind is clear of guilt.

The purpose of the past two devotionals is to aid parents in dealing with the root of a child's problems rather than the fruit. If we concentrate on their misbehavior, their sullen spirit, their temper, or their dislike for looking us in the eye, we will never correct the problem! Those are only outward signs of a deeper problem. Somewhere within there is a sin that must be cleansed. It may be a sin of which the child is unaware—a failure to forgive someone for an offense or bitterness for what they consider a past injustice against them. Or it may be a secret sin weighing heavily on the mind. Either way, the wise parent will dig for the root of the problem, not simply put a band-aid on the symptom.

Final thought: Behind the fruit lies the root. Dig for it with probing questions.

Day 160

PROVERBS 28:5

"Evil men understand not judgment: but they that seek the Lord understand all things."

Wisdom in Education

True education is God-focused. Only he who knows the Lord is capable of teaching truth, and if truth is not taught, education has not taken place.

True education sees God in every discipline of study whether math, the sciences, grammar, literature, sociology, history, geography, or health.

A few weeks ago we saw God in a leaf. He is also in the sun, in the perfect order of mathematics, and in the laws of grammar. History is His story. Geography is by His design. He is the plumb line by which all literature must be judged. To teach these disciplines apart from God is not to educate but to delude!

There is no history or science without Him. Only if you seek to portray His character and majesty in every discipline you teach, do you truly understand what you teach! Just as the Pharisees searched the Scriptures (John 5:39) but failed to see Jesus, so we may study our subject well yet fail to see the Lord in it!

This is yet another reason parents should seriously consider providing their children with a Christ-centered education. In a real sense, a godless education is no education at all! Do your child's teachers "seek the Lord" in all that they teach? Do you as a parent take the time to show your children the glory of God in every field of learning?

Final thought: If your child does not see God in every subject learned, he has not truly been taught!

Day 161

PROVERBS 28:13

"He that covereth his sins shall not prosper: but whoso confesseth and forsaketh them shall have mercy."

Wisdom in Honesty

Honesty is of paramount importance in reaching youth. Youth are brutally honest—ranging from vulgarity to spilling their guts. They hate pretense. The 1960s revolution was to some extent a rebellion against what the younger generation saw as gross hypocrisy in the American political and economic systems. Yet, youth are sometimes the greatest pretenders in society! They cover up sin with politeness and feigned innocence. They have two standards: what they expect from adults and what they do when in trouble.

Of course, God has a standard too. His standard is holiness or righteousness. Both terms imply the absence of impurity (including all forms of deception) and the presence of righteous behavior. God will give mercy to those who honestly admit and forsake their sins.

We please both God and man when we are honest. Yet, parents sometimes use arguments against various sins that don't hold water. When children challenge those fallacious arguments, don't be a hard head! Admit the fallacy! That doesn't mean the sin is right; it just means one of your arguments wasn't credible. By admitting it, you gain your child's confidence. By refusing to be honest, you lose your credibility.

Final thought: Children will listen better to the parent who admits, "I don't know" or "I was wrong" than to the parent who is always right!

"He that rebuketh a man afterwards shall find more favour than he that flattereth with the tongue."

Wisdom in Godly Rebuke

Rebuke is rarely easy for the giver or the receiver. However, afterwards (sometimes long afterwards) the person learns to appreciate the friend who had the courage to rebuke him and save him from a world of harm.

The Complete Biblical Library points out the danger of choosing flattery over rebuke: "Flattery will not help a child. Solomon portrays flattery as lying with evil intent (Prov. 26:28), but it can also be simply telling someone what they want to hear." Either way, the flattery does more harm than good.

The Hebrew word for *rebuke* means to convict in the legal sense. It is to show the offender, through powerful scriptural arguments, that he is wrong and that his sin will cost him dearly. It is not the same as fussing, nor is it the same as venting your anger on your child's misdeeds. It is not ranting and raving.

Biblical rebuke is counseling. It is calmly and kindly using the Bible to show a child that he is a sinner, showing him the true name of his sin (lying, stealing, dishonesty, greed, judging others, gossip, adultery, drunkenness), and showing him the penalty for his sin. When rebuke is given using Scripture, it convinces the youth of his sin, humbles him before God, and leads him to confession. Biblical rebuke should be followed by "instruction in righteousness"—giving biblical steps to overcome sin (2 Tim. 3:16).

Final thought: Do you rant and rave, or do you rebuke? Only the latter, done with the Bible in hand, will prosper your child.

Day 163

PROVERBS 28:26
"He that trusteth in his own heart is a fool: but whoso walketh wisely, he shall be delivered."

Wisdom in Self-Distrust

The flesh trusts nothing but itself! We have a natural distrust of everything but self. Some can't relax when others drive the car. Some can't designate responsibility because no one else could do it right. Over time we learn to trust our own judgment, wisdom, experience, and decision-making. This is seen in how little we pray or how seldom we seek the advice of others!

And yet, our heart is a deceiver. The Bible says it is desperately wicked. "To trust an imposter, who has deceived us a hundred times, or a traitor, who has proved himself false to our best interests, is surely to deserve the name of fool" (Charles Bridges). Yet, how often do we trust our heart?

Israel defeated Jericho with fear and trembling and by seeking God's face. Next they faced Ai. But there was no fear, or trembling, or prayer! They knew what to do. They had beaten a much stronger enemy at Jericho. They trusted their experience and their superior numbers and were shamefully defeated!

The more experience we have, the less we pray. We have learned the "best" way. We have been down this road before. We know how to parent! We discipline (or fail to discipline) our children based on past experience, common sense, or what we think is good judgment. So, we don't pray! How much prayer goes into the daily handling of your child's life?

Final thought: How little we pray is a measure of how big a fool we are! The wisest parents spend much time on their knees.

Day 164

PROVERBS 29:2

"When the righteous are in authority, the people rejoice: but when the wicked beareth rule, the people mourn."

Wisdom in Righteousness

Are you a righteous parent? A righteous parent has trusted Christ as His Lord and Savior and has had the righteousness of Christ imputed (charged) to his account. Righteous parents imitate Christ and are obedient to the Word. Righteous parents are compassionate as Christ was compassionate. They are honest and transparent as Christ was honest. They are gentle, even as Christ of whom it was said, "A bruised reed shall he not break, and smoking flax shall he not quench" (Matt. 12:20). Children flocked to Him because there was no fear of what He might say or do.

Righteous parents produce a happy child who does not need to be fearful. The child knows she will not be reprimanded for questions she asks or answers she gives. She can tell her darkest thoughts and know her parents will still accept her.

Righteous parents through their love produce happy children. The children trust their parents' chastening because the parents exercise self-control and gentleness even in times of correction. Righteous parents go the second mile to help their children understand. They are compassionate.

Righteous parents produce happy children because their children admire their wisdom and know their parents back up their words with Scripture. Wise parents quickly admit mistakes and ask forgiveness when they are wrong. The children can see that their parents are honest and humble.

Final thought: Righteous parents make a happy home!

Day 165

PROVERBS 29:11

"A fool uttereth all his mind: but a wise man keepeth it in till afterwards."

Wisdom in Controlling the Tongue

Solomon writes elsewhere: "To everything there is a season, and a time to every purpose under the heaven…a time to keep silent, and a time to speak" (Eccles. 3:1, 7). The control of the tongue is a test of character and wise timing.

The man who speaks hastily is most often proud and foolish. Yet, he thinks himself to be honest! He says what's on his mind—nothing is hidden. But his rash words actually prove his lack of wisdom and good sense and the depth of his folly!

Pride speaks quickly because it assumes omniscience. It proclaims, "I don't need to think; I intuitively know what is right." A man hasty in speech does not consider the fact that a deceptive heart controls his mind.

Conversely, humility prays and thinks before it speaks. It admits that we don't know as we should know. It recognizes the omniscience of God and seeks His mind before addressing the situation.

But is it not dishonest to withhold what we think? We should never speak against our mind, but we don't always have to speak our whole mind. Be careful to speak nothing but the truth. But the whole truth may sometimes be restrained (see 1 Sam. 16:1–2).

Final thought: Think and pray before you speak. Speak only what is necessary.

Day 166

PROVERBS 29:15

"The rod and reproof give wisdom: but a child left to himself bringeth his mother to shame."

Wisdom in Instructive Discipline

The rod without reproof hardens the heart. Reproof without the rod hardens the will. Yet when combined, they soften both the heart and the will!

Eli reproved his sons but spared the rod (1 Sam. 2:22–25; 3:13). The result was two sons with hardened wills and ultimately untimely deaths. The child who gets his own way without restraint becomes an ill-functioning adult. The temper that was thought so cute as a child will harden and strengthen as an adult.

Others use the rod but spare the reproof. They are quick to punish. They are quick to scold and rage. Yet, they fail to carefully lead their child verse by verse through a discussion of his sin.

Reproof takes time. Impatient parents often rush to punish but offer little counsel. The goal is immediate conformity with scarce thought given to using the child's failure as a teaching opportunity. But growth is a process requiring someone who cares enough to correct with the Word and wait for the results. We would rather use the immediacy of the rod than the time consuming commitment of reproof. The rod requires little effort, time, or thought, but reproof requires all three.

Final thought: Do you take the easy way out and punish rather than counsel? The child without both will bring his home to shame.

Day 167

PROVERBS 29:15

"The rod and reproof give wisdom: but a child left to himself bringeth his mother to shame."

Wisdom in Giving Reproof

It is not enough to discipline children, we must disciple them! Discipleship certainly includes the discipline, but it must also include reproof or biblical admonition. Lou Priolo, in his excellent book, *Teach Them Diligently*, asks six probing questions concerning the extent to which parents minister the Word to their children. We would do well to ask these questions of ourselves.

1. How well do you know the Scriptures yourself?
2. How often do you refer to the Bible in the course of normal conversation with your children?
3. How adept are you at teaching and relating the Scriptures to them in everyday life?
4. How effectively do you use the Scriptures to reprove (convict) them of their sin? (Do you reprove in such a way that causes them to revere God's Word or to disdain it?)
5. How consistently do you use the Bible when you correct them?
6. How do you use the Bible to train your children in righteousness to help them to do better in the future?

Final thought: It is our joy to both know and use the Scriptures as God intended. Scripture alone is sufficient for the life and godliness of our children (2 Pet. 1:3).

Day 168

PROVERBS 29:18

"Where there is no vision, the people perish: but he that keepeth the law, happy is he."

Wisdom in Using the Word

This verse is among the most misunderstood verses in Scripture. Missionaries often use it to remind us that we need a vision for missions, or the lost will perish. While we do need a vision for the lost, that is not the teaching of this verse! The vision spoken of here is specifically the revelation of God in the Word. When God revealed Himself in the Old Testament, He did so by visions, dreams, and specific revelation. As long as God revealed Himself to prophets, the people had hope—God was still speaking, giving visions, and caring for His people. But when God grew silent and no more visions were given, the people were doomed.

Children need a vision of a great and awesome God that will transform their lives.

When parents magnify the God of the Word in daily conversation, the children have hope. But when parents rely on medication, on rules (even Biblical ones), on psychology, or on strict discipline more than on a transforming vision of their glorious God, their children will perish!

We must come to grips with the glory of God in dealing with children's hearts. Rules and harsh discipline may temporarily change behavior, but they are not designed to change the heart! Only when children are led to see "the breadth and length, and height and depth" of "the love of God" can we capture their minds and imagination and give them a heart for God that will transform their lives. Are you so taken with the glory of your Savior, that your children fall in love with Him and want to please Him, or do you, rather, correct with godless discipline?

Final thought: The power to change a life is in a vision of the glory and grace of God not in simple conformity to Biblical rules.

Day 169

PROVERBS 29:26

"Many seek the ruler's favor; but every man's judgment cometh from the Lord."

Wisdom in Pleasing Him

Seek God to be your friend! His favor is for a lifetime (Ps. 30:5). Sadly, we seek the favor of friends and authorities ("many seek the ruler's favor") yet neglect the favor of the only One "with whom we have to do" (Heb. 4:13)!

It is God alone who will ultimately judge us. "But every man's judgment cometh from the Lord." Should we not seek to please Him above all others? Do we not ultimately work for Him? Will the ultimate reward not be handed out at His throne? If only we would live each day with eternity's values in view! Our goal should not be to teach or even to change our children's lives. Our ultimate goal should be to please our Heavenly Judge!

How do we please the ultimate Judge of all the earth? Not by "doing right" alone. Doing what is right alone does not please Him. With what is He pleased? He is pleased when…

- …our hearts are filled with Him (Ps. 1:1–2).
- …our life is godly (Ps. 51:19).
- …we fear Him—are in loving awe of Him (Ps. 112:1; 128:1).
- …we hear Him; we daily watch at His gates and wait at His doors (Prov. 8:34).

Final thought: Cultivate friendship with God above pleasing man. He is the ultimate rewarder of those that please Him.

Day 170

PROVERBS 30:5-6

"Every word of God is pure: he is a shield unto them that put their trust in him. Add thou not unto his words lest he reprove thee, and thou be found a liar."

Wisdom in Using God's Word

God's Word is pure. It has stood the trial, and no dross has been found in it. Critics, scholars, nations, and time each added fuel to the fires of testing. Though they sought to find the dross, they found only that God's Word is without error. If every word of God is tested and proven true, we must put our total trust in Him. "All scripture is…profitable for doctrine, for reproof, for correction, for instruction in, that the man of God may be perfect, thoroughly furnished unto all good works" (2 Tim. 3:16–17).

Do we truly believe that God's Word is all we need to produce godly youth, or do we add unto his words? Sadly, some parents seek to manipulate youth or to enforce godliness by rules (not that rules are wrong—they are necessary—but they have nothing to do with producing godliness). Others accept the theories of clinical psychologists that problems are due to chemical imbalances or emotional scars that must be cured by medication. Yet, these theories and mental diseases or disorders have never been medically proven. Sadly, we leave the Bible on the shelf and go to the medicine cabinet or the rulebook to correct today's youth!

Final thought: God's Word is sufficient for "all things that pertain unto life and godliness through the knowledge of Him" (2 Pet. 1:3). Use it to know Him!

Day 171

"Who can find a virtuous woman? For her price is far above rubies. The heart of her husband doth safely trust in her, so that he shall have no need of spoil. She will do him good and not evil all the days of her life."

Virtuous Parents Are Faithful

These last ten days will deal with aspects of the virtuous parent. We will use the passage on the virtuous woman in Proverbs 31 as our text. Though this passage describes the godly wife, we beg permission to apply it to both parents. Should we not all have these qualities? Are they reserved only for moms? Virtuous dads will have these same qualities.

This passage is an elegant poem of twenty-two verses with each verse beginning with one of the successive letters of the Hebrew alphabet. So rare is the virtuous woman that the poem begins with the challenge, "Who can find a virtuous woman?" So it may be said of both parents. Where are our virtuous parents? Is not their price far above rubies?

The first characteristic is faithfulness. Those around her trust her and know that she will do them good. Her husband is at ease while gone. His comfort and success is her highest happiness. The children of such parents trust in them, knowing their parents will do them good. Likewise, each spouse rests assured that their partner's greatest burden is the welfare of the child!

Final thought: A faithful parent works tirelessly to one end—to see her children mature in the Lord.

Day 172

PROVERBS 31:13

"She seeketh wool, and flax, and worketh willingly with her hands."

Virtuous Parents Are Industrious

Throughout this passage the energy and work ethic of the virtuous woman are evident. Manual labor, menial service, and self-denial characterize the virtuous. So it is with both parents.

Each day we work with the fabric of our child's life. We weave a life that will in the end reflect the glory of God. There is no time for laziness. Every day is an opportunity. We will only have our children a few short years, and then they will move on in life! As the virtuous woman seeketh wool and flax, so must we seek to bring just the right touch to each child. Some need one cloth, some another. Some need the harsh shades of correction and discipline; some need the pastels of a softer, kinder word. Whatever the case, each requires work. A parent can ill-afford to let their child sit day after day and not progress spiritually. She must not trivialize the child's failures, faults, sins, and talents. Each must be energetically worked with her hands.

There is no place for laziness in God's business. Paul commands us to be "not slothful in business; fervent in spirit; serving the Lord" (Rom. 12:11). The last phrase is the key to industry—we serve the Lord! Our love for Him should drive us even more than our love for our children! He is too precious to waste a day. His work is the greatest work. We are about the Father's business!

Final thought: Flaming hearts for God produce unflagging hands for our children.

Day 173

PROVERBS 31:14

"She is like the merchants' ships; she bringeth her food from afar."

Virtuous Parents Are Resourceful

A virtuous wife is resourceful. She does whatever is necessary to provide for the needs of those she loves. As merchant ships bring goods from afar, so she constantly searches for provisions for her family.

A virtuous dad has these same qualities. He looks for ways to meet the needs of his children. One mom read *Sports Illustrated* for examples and illustrations to which her boy could relate. Another collected huge leaves while sightseeing in Oregon to teach the lesson on leaves from this devotional. The world around us is a rich revelation of the glory of God. Resourceful parents will use whatever is at hand to instill a heart for God in their children.

The resourcefulness of the virtuous mom and dad is driven by their relationship with the Lord (Prov. 31:30). The more they fear the Lord (see Him in everything they read or see), the more resources they find to magnify Him. David speaks of God enlarging his heart (Ps. 119:32), that is, giving him a greater capacity to see and know the Lord. Our hearts and minds are like ships. They must be enlarged with wisdom—gathered from the shores of meditation and prayer. The greater our capacity to see the Lord in the world around us and in his Word, the easier it is to return with "ships" (hearts) laden with treasure to bestow on our children.

Final thought: The virtuous parent enlarges his heart to see the wonders of God in the world and in the Word bringing those resources daily to his family.

Day 174

PROVERBS 31:15

"She riseth also while it is yet night, and giveth meat to her household, and a portion to her maidens."

Virtuous Parents Are Disciplined

Virtuous wives are disciplined. They are not only careful to seek what is best, but they discipline themselves to meet the needs of their family before daybreak. Old Testament wives did not have electricity! What they accomplished was done in the precious hours of daylight. Thus, they rose before sunup to feed their families and maids and gave them their assignments. They could then give the daylight hours to work in the fields.

Does this not apply to dads as well? A godly dad rises earlier than others that he might spend time with the Lord before his family wakes. He knows that his own heart must be fed and his mind given proper instructions from the Lord. The time he must spend at work will not allow him the luxury of time with the Lord. Thus, he must prepare spiritual food while it is yet night. Then he will have something with which to feed his children that evening!

Such a life requires discipline. Susanna Wesley (who had 22 children) arose at 4:00 am to spend an hour or more with the Lord before her children awoke. Such discipline was rewarded with godly children, two of which, John and Charles, still impact the world (two hundred years later) through their songs and writings!

Final thought: What we do before we go to work may be more important than what we do at work!

Day 175

PROVERBS 31:16

"She considereth a field, and buyeth it: with the fruit of her hands she planteth a vineyard."

Virtuous Parents Are Cultivators

The virtuous woman is an astute real estate appraiser! She carefully studies property and wisely chooses the field she thinks is best for a vineyard. After making her decision, she purchases the field and just as carefully works the field with her own hands to insure a rich harvest.

Likewise, the goal of a virtuous parent is to produce a crop of mature, godly children. But such a goal is only realized through hours of toil and care. First, the virtuous parent considers the field (in this case, the hearts of her children). She studies their likes, dislikes, aptitudes, successes, sins, and weaknesses. She desires to sow on fertile ground. Each "field" is different. She will not work by impulse but by purpose. She considers each field. She looks at the soil of the heart so she can be most effective in each life. One likes sports, so she will use sports terminology; another learns visually, so she will draw pictures and diagrams; a third child is starved for assurance, so she will give him special attention. She considers each child.

Virtuous parents also "plant" with their hands. They are personally involved in the life of each child. They cheer for them, counsel with them, eat meals with them, and play with them. My virtuous woman (my wife) has toiled a lifetime for our children. She attended every play, every ballgame, and every recital. She counseled each one endlessly in our kitchen while preparing meals! She took an interest in each child's endeavors whether cheerleading, swimming, gymnastics, medicine, preaching, piano, guitar, voice, hunting, guns, fishing, or doll collecting.

Final thought: Those who cultivate hearts produce a rich harvest.

Day 176

PROVERBS 31:17
"She girdeth her loins with strength, and strengtheneth her arms."

Virtuous Parents Stay in Shape

A virtuous wife is concerned for her health because her family needs her. She exercises. She is careful of her weight and her stamina. Not that she is vain, but she knows that her health is vital to the welfare of her home. Her children need her energy. Her husband needs her vitality. When Mom is sick, so is the whole household!

The virtuous dad should also be concerned with his health. He believes so strongly in the value of his labor that he diligently strengthens himself for the task. When the health is gone, the opportunity for service is gone! When the energy is gone, the vineyard dries. He must be strong to work in the field each day.

The Bible speaks of two types of health: physical and spiritual (1 Tim. 4:8; 3 John 2). Though godly health is paramount, physical well-being is also necessary. Both must be nurtured that the servant of God might be better able to serve.

Godly exercise includes daily meditation on God in the Word, prayer, Bible study, witnessing, and faithfully serving those God brings into your life (your children in particular).

Physical exercise is also vital. A virtuous parent will not be slovenly in "girding his loins with strength." He will watch his weight and keep himself fit—for the sake of his Lord, as well as his family! Both his spiritual and physical regimen is designed to better prepare him to serve the Lord.

Final thought: An unfit parent may reveal a selfish parent!

Day 177

PROVERBS 31:19-20

"She layeth her hands to the spindle, and her hands hold the distaff. She stretcheth out her hand to the poor; yea, she reacheth forth her hands to the needy."

Virtuous Parents Are Energetically Compassionate

These two verses seem to address two different subjects: industry (v. 19) and compassion (v. 20). Yet they are linked by four parallel phrases: "she layeth her hands" (v. 19) with "she stretcheth out her hand" (v. 20); and "her hands hold" (v. 19) with "she reacheth forth her hands" (v. 20). This structure reveals the close connection between industry and compassion. Only the compassionate have the energy to give themselves for others! Laziness seldom shows kindness or concern. While laziness dulls the mind and drains energy, love sharpens both.

Love energized the virtuous woman. She spent long hours at the loom making garments for her family. Compassionate parents work tirelessly for their children. Compassion motivates them to meet each child's needs. Compassion thinks of ways to make the home a spiritual haven. Compassion creates new ideas to teach children the truths of God's Word. Compassion talks gently with children, prays with children, spends extra time with struggling youth, and doesn't quit because she is tired! Compassion never fails (quits)! Her palms, though tired, still grasp the distaff. Dad comes home from work wanting to spend time with his children rather than turning on the TV or disappearing into the garage.

Final thought: Love energizes and tirelessly sacrifices to reach each child.

Day 178

"She is not afraid of the snow for her household: for all her household are clothed with scarlet."

Virtuous Parents Prepare Children for Winter

Your children must be prepared for a dangerous future! Sin and temptation—disguised to deceive—wait around the corner. Divorce, immorality, a cut-throat business world, terrorism, liberal theology, and a world gone mad seek to pull youth into their devouring vortex. Only the most careful parent can say with confidence, "I am not afraid for my children—for I have given them all they need for the snow of life."

As the virtuous woman prepared her children for the harsh realities of winter, so the virtuous parent must prepare his children for the harsh realities they will face. He realizes that sin lies in each child's heart and seeks to wash it white as snow with the scarlet blood of Christ. Further, he knows that even saved youth struggle with the flesh. Anger, bitterness, pride, greed, an unforgiving spirit, and a myriad of other sins lie as sleeping beasts in the heart of each child. Youth must learn how to biblically deal with each. Virtuous parents show them how. Children must be challenged to analyze each TV program, each movie, and every circumstance in life in light of what the Bible teaches. They must be taught the consequences of sin in the lives of Biblical characters and be shown how kings who "did not seek the Lord" found God's judgment (study 1, 2 Chron.). If we fail to so teach our children, we fail to give them scarlet garments for the winter!

Final thought: Virtuous parents prepare their children to overcome the beasts crouching in their own hearts.

Day 179

"She maketh herself coverings of tapestry; her clothing is silk and purple. Her husband is known in the gates, when he sitteth among the elders of the land."

Virtuous Parents Dress Appropriately

The virtuous woman is concerned with her appearance because it is a reflection on her husband. Silk and purple bespoke dignity and wellbeing for her husband who is known in the gates, when he sits among the elders of the land. To be unkempt or slovenly would disgrace her earthly lord—a thing she was loath to do.

Likewise, the virtuous parent would dress to honor his Lord. A disheveled or sloppy appearance might reflect a careless concern for God's glory! Though Scripture reminds us that God looks on the heart, it also reveals that God is concerned with our appearance! Though He may not care about our physical looks, He is interested in our attire! Modesty, cleanliness, order, and appropriateness of dress are principles God lays down in His Word.

However, there is another type of clothing that should concern us—our spiritual attire! The Bible often speaks of things we are to put on: "robes of righteousness" (Isa. 61:10), "the armor of God" (Eph. 6:10, 13), "armor of light" (Rom. 13:12), "mercy, kindness, humility, meekness, longsuffering, love" (Col. 3:12, 14), and a "meek and quiet spirit" (1 Pet. 3:4). Virtuous parents must be careful to "put on" such clothing each day while also taking pains to "put off" clothing which detracts from the glory of God—anger, wrath, malice, slander, abusive speech, lying, and other such sins (Col. 3:8-9).

Parents who detract from the glory of God by their "spiritual clothing" will produce children who likewise dishonor their God.

Final thought: If you are a "child of the King," show your children how His children "dress."

Day 180

PROVERBS 31:28
"Her children arise up, and call her blessed; her husband also, and he praiseth her."

The Virtuous Parent Is Blessed

So wise and godly is the virtuous woman that both her children and her husband honor and praise her. Her sacrifice is rewarded. The burning of midnight oil, the candle that goeth not out by night, and the selfless life produce grateful children and a thankful husband.

The virtuous parent is also blessed. Her blessings are not measured in dollars and cents but in something far more valuable—in lives that are forever changed and in a Lord who is well pleased! Paul said, "For what is our hope, or joy, or crown of rejoicing? Are not even ye in the presence of our Lord Jesus Christ at his coming?" (1 Thess. 2:19). Is this not our joy as well?

I praise a Mom who sacrificed time and health for me. I praise a Mom who loved the Lord with every ounce of energy in her body. I praise a Mom who was always happy, who never complained, and who showed the love of Christ. I praise a mom who "dressed" in the silks of joy, sacrifice, purity, love for God, righteousness, and praise. My Mom lived a life of boundless energy for both her family and her Lord.

I praise a Dad who lived a humble, consistent, and godly life. I praise a Dad who diligently taught me the Word, prayed for me, and taught me to see the glory of God in things as diverse as a spider, the sunset, and the stars. He dressed in robes of righteousness, faithfulness to the Word, and a love for the Lord.

Because of their lives, their son grew up to love their God and to attempt to so teach his children—and to write this book. I pray my children will so love the same Lord through my life.

Final thought: How will your children remember you? What "god/God" will they follow?

APPENDIX

Psalm 91

1   He that dwelleth in the secret place of the Most High (El Elyon) shall abide under the shadow of the Almighty (El Shaddai).

2   I will say of the LORD (Yahweh/Jehovah), He is my refuge and my fortress: my God (Elohim) in him will I trust.

3   Surely he shall deliver thee from the snare of the fowler, and from the noisome pestilence.

4   He shall cover thee with his feathers, and under his wings shalt thou trust: his truth shall be thy shield and buckler.

5   Thou shalt not be afraid for the terror by night; nor for the arrow that flieth by day.

. . .

9   Because thou hast made the LORD (Yahweh/Jehovah), which is my refuge, even the Most High (El Elyon) thy habitation;

10   There shall no evil befall thee, neither shall any plague come nigh thy dwelling.

11   For he shall give his angels charge over thee, to keep thee in all thy ways.

12   They shall bear thee up in their hands, lest thou dash thy foot against a stone.

. . .

God says:

14   Because he (the believer) hath set his love upon me (God), therefore will I deliver him: I will set him on high because he hath known my name.

Names of God

Teach your children the names of God and their meanings. Then as a family, practice using these names in the suggested situations. As your children hear you invoking God's names for different situations, they will learn to use God's name as a strong tower in time of trouble.

Name of God	Meaning of the Name	Use of the Name
El, Elohim (el-lo-heem')	The Strong One	When I feel helpless and weak; when I need strength
El Shaddai (el shad-di')	All Sufficient God	When I have a desperate need
El Elyon (el el-yon')	Most High God (He is stronger than Satan and my enemies)	When I am under attack by Satan or others; when I am afraid
El Roi (el ro-i')	God who sees	When I am tempted to sin in private; when I feel no one knows about my hurt or problems
Jehovah, Yahweh, Lord (je-ho'-vah, yah'-weh)	The Self-Existent One (Speaks of his intimate relationship with man)	When I feel no one cares
Jehovah Shammah (je-ho'-vah sham'-mah)	The Lord is present	When I feel alone
Jehovah Jirah (je-ho'-vah ji'-rah)	The Lord will provide	When I have a desperate need
Jehovah Nissi (je-ho'-vah nis'-si)	The Lord my banner	When I am tempted to not stand for Christ
Jehovah M'Kaddesh (je-ho'-vah m'-kad'-ish)	The Lord is Holy	When I am tempted to sin
Adonai (a-do-ni')	Master, Lord	When I am tempted to run my own life; when I need guidance

Additional Resources

Positive Action For Christ offers many resources that can help your family become more God-focused as you behold His glory and grace together.

The Pursuit of God by A. W. Tozer

This book shows that man can know, in a very personal way, our Mejestic God. It aims to inspire the reader in a lifelong personal discipleship of pursuing God. It can be read individually or together as a family. Either way, this book is certain to be a blessing.

Christ Precious to Those Who Believe by John Fawcett

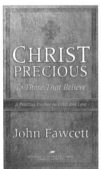

Fawcett wrote this work to instill in his readers "a sincere attachment to the Author of Salvation." There are many things in this world that people hold precious, but Christ is shown here to outshine them all.

Apples for Teachers by Frank Hamrick

In this devotional, Frank Hamrick discusses many of the same passages covered in *Wisdom for Parents* from the prespective of a classroom instead of the home. Written to encourage teachers and to focus their hearts and minds on God, this book would make a wonderful gift for your children's teachers.

The Heart of the Matter by Frank Hamrick

Have you ever wondered what the ultimate goal should be in training your children? Frank Hamrick looks at the question in the setting of a Christian School. He proves that the purpose of Christian education is not to teach young people how to live but to teach them to magnify the majesty of God.

For more information or to receive a catalog, please visit us at www.positiveaction.org or call (800) 688–3008.